Weight and Strength Training for Kids and Teenagers

Weight and Strength Training for Kids and Teenagers

A Responsible Guide for Parents, Teachers, Coaches, and Young Athletes

Ken and Chris Sprague

Foreword by John D. Polansky, M.D.

Jeremy P. Tarcher, Inc.
Los Angeles

To Donna Wong,
a one-in-a-million wife and mom
whose love and companionship enrich our lives
and who was an indispensable
collaborator in writing
this book.

Library of Congress Cataloging-in-Publication Data

Sprague, Ken.
    Weight and strength training for kids and teen-
agers : a responsible guide for parents, teachers,
coaches, and young athletes / by Ken Sprague and
Chris Sprague. — First ed.
        p.   cm.
    Includes bibliographical reference and index.
    ISBN 0-87477-643-0 : $12.95
    1. Weight training for children.   2. Exercise for
children.
I. Sprague, Chris.   II. Title.
GV546.6.C45S68   1991   91-9448
796.41—dc20   CIP

Manufactured in the United States of America
10   9   8   7   6   5   4   3   2   1

First Edition

Jeremy P. Tarcher, Inc.
5858 Wilshire Blvd., Suite 200
Los Angeles, California 90036

Distributed by St. Martin's Press, New York

Design by Deborah Daly
Photographs including cover by John Bauguess
Illustrations by Kiki Metzler

Contents

Part One: Addressing Your Concerns   1

Part Two: As You Start   35

Chapter 5: Basics   37

Chapter 6: Setting Up a Home Gym   47

Chapter 7: Weight Training and Nutrition   55

Acknowledgments

Topping the list of acknowledgments is Jeremy Tarcher,—a fellow weight trainer and longtime friend—whose professional wisdom and direction positively impacted the project from creation to conclusion. Every author should be so lucky.

Naturally, a wise publisher surrounds himself with good in-house people. A special thanks to those on his staff that we've had the opportunity to work with: Daniel Malvin for editorial administration, Deborah Daly for art direction and design, Paul Murphy for layout and production editing, Michael Dougherty for publicity, and Lisa Chadwick for administrative assistance.

Also thanks to Marian Castinado for her general but thorough editorial assistance and timely, on-target suggestions. Thank you to Dr. John Polansky for special editorial assistance and meticulous attention throughout preparation of the manuscript.

Thank you to Jennifer Waldrop, Kevin Rutell, Dusty Sprague, Dusty Kinman, Beth Ratliff, Sherry Harris, Amy Oland, Jonah Whitten, Donna Wong, John Lassen, Yeritza Figueroa, Angela Etter, Bobby Lamar, Jocelyn Lamar, Sylvie Florendo, and Marielle Florendo for modeling for the exercise demonstrations. And thanks to Ron Finne, Mary Lorence, Judy Wade, and Brian Romine for help organizing the photo sessions of an exceptionally gifted photographer, John Bauguess.

Thanks for the cover shot goes to Southside Fitness Club and Carole Kabot; the models are Robert Hausmann, Brandon Hausmann, Katie Polansky, Kristi Yim, Jennifer Waldrop, and Kevin Rutell. And thanks to John Bauguess who took the picture.

A special note of appreciation to Jon and Gene Joseph of Pacific Nautilus, Mark Delp, Melissa Christensen, and V. Pat Lombardi for support, encouragement, and inspiration provided to young and old athletes and students.

Foreword

Weight training for kids? You have got to be kidding! No, I'm not. Read on.

The importance of exercise in maintaining good health for people of all ages is becoming increasingly recognized. It is no coincidence that President Bush has named Arnold Schwarzenegger chairman of the President's Council on Physical Fitness. When should one begin to learn about fitness and make a commitment to it? The answer is: earlier than we ever imagined.

Kids are interested in strength. The superheroes that fill children's books have captivated kids' attention for decades. How can children achieve an increase in their own strength? Weight training is a very good way.

This book addresses the concerns that parents will have if their children desire to begin weight training. It tells how to safely begin, how to make weight training a shared activity between parent and child, and describes the benefits, both physical and psychological, for kids (and parents too).

After more than twenty years of practicing medicine, I am more impressed than ever with the role of fitness in overall well-being. I am so pleased to see exercise in general, and weight training in particular, come from relative obscurity to a prominent place in American life. Coaches have introduced weight training into the preparation for almost every sport. Now the benefits of childhood conditioning are beginning to be appreciated.

As a father of an eleven-year-old son and an eight-year-old daughter, I am aware of my children's desires to be good athletes. How to help them make the most of their potential is of great interest to me. Guiding them to develop good eating and exercise habits can be educational for the children, healthy for the parents, and fun for both.

This book addresses the special relationship parents and children can have in doing an exercise program together. It's good for building that important sense of self-esteem children get when they do something for themselves. There are no failures in weight training, only progressive levels of success. What a wonderful noncompetitive activity for parents and children to do together!

As parents look for new ideas to help their children grow psychologically as well as physically, this book will provide direction for a healthy activity than can be shared and enjoyed on almost any level. The facts that you need to begin are presented in an easily understandable, informative, and entertaining style. The unexpected benefit that comes from beginning this program with your children is the togetherness you will feel in sharing their delight.

JOHN D. POLANSKY, M.D.

A Message to Parents and Coaches

Weight training has been part of my life for thirty-five years. As a skinny ten-year-old, I tagged along to the local YMCA's weight room with my older brother. In retrospect, I see that those early trips were the beginning of an athletic career and occupational pursuit that would be based on the joys and accomplishments of weight training.

The ensuing years of effort in the weight room produced tangible rewards. The first was my improved sports performance, which in turn led to a college scholarship in track and field. Later, I owned and operated the original and world-famous Gold's Gym—the training ground for such muscular giants as Arnold Schwarzenegger, Lou Ferrigno, and Hulk Hogan.

Life came full circle when I heard another ten-year-old boy's casual request to tag along to the gym: It was from my son, Chris, and it became the impetus for this book.

Our father-and-son adventure into weight training has turned out to be far more interesting, intellectually demanding, and emotionally rewarding than I could possibly have expected. Chris and I became a regular team in the weight room. We enjoyed training together, mutually benefiting from the camaraderie as much as from the physical activity.

Within months, he was pressing 600 pounds with his legs—fifteen times per set. Child or adult, that's a lot of weight. So much that I became concerned. Could lifting weights harm Chris? He had shown no obvious ill-effects, but gym banter suggested that weight training was bad for kids. I had to be sure.

Trips to the local bookstores did not solve my dilemma. Of the many books on weight training for adults, not one answered the important questions about its effects on children. Based on the lack of practical information, you'd think that children did not weight train. Yet from practical experience I knew that was not true. Countless children weight train in family garages, school gymnasiums, and as tagalongs.

Finding no help in the marketplace, I closeted myself in university research libraries for months on end seeking answers to questions that centered on one theme: Is weight training safe and effective for children and young adults?

This book recounts the answers that I found. In brief, adult training programs are not appropriate for children. Their bodies are different from adults'; they have special needs. The specifics of their muscles, bones, and hormones must be factored into the training programs. Nevertheless, young people do want to train, and can do so safely.

For kids already involved in, or about to start, weight training, this book can serve as a responsible guide to a safe, effective program designed specifically for children and teenagers. The information you'll find here is based on the most up-to-date scientific research as well as my many years of personal experience.

Many of the chapters are written as questions and answers—on the same issues that I wrestled with when my son took a serious interest in weight training. What worried me then has evaporated in the light of scientific research, and I now train with my son according to the concepts and programs found in this book. I am certain that they are safe and effective for him, and I can conscientiously recommend the programs to your children or students.

May this book be a solid first step to a lifetime exercise program!

KEN SPRAGUE

A Message to Kids

Hi! My name is Chris and I'm eleven years old. I want to tell you about how I got into weight training. I was first interested in weight training because I noticed that every big guy I know of lifts weights, and I want to be strong like them. Every kid I know wants to weightlift, and the kids who do really stand out in sports.

Second, my dad lifts weights. So one day I just asked if I could go along to the gym and have him show me what to do. It was so much fun that I knew right away I would continue weight training forever! It's also a real challenge. You can work as much as you want, to build the kind of body you want.

Another good reason I love weight training is the results. I'm stronger; I have more power. Things are a lot easier to lift. Also, I see my body change and shape up. My arms feel and look strong, and my legs are powerful. And when I play sports, I don't get tired as fast as I used to. It helps me shoot baskets and defend against players in football.

I enjoy doing the different weight training exercises. I've even developed a grunt when I lift. I go at it as hard as I can. I know it's safe as long as I watch my form during the exercises, so I don't hold back.

What's really great is that my dad gets inspired seeing me work, and that makes him train harder. We're a real team! I always look forward to weight training, and so will you. Especially after you see the results!

Have a great workout! Write to me and tell me how you like weight training.

Your new friend,

Chris Sprague

CHRIS SPRAGUE

Part One

Addressing Your Concerns

Chapter 1

The Biggest Questions

Weight training, a form of exercise in which hand-held weights or a machine provide resistance as a person moves, has been a popular way for adults to stay healthy and fit since the early 1980s. Millions have done it, including sports and entertainment celebrities such as Jane Fonda, Bo Jackson, José Canseco, Madonna, and Michael Jordan—to name just a few. Besides the rich and famous, millions of moms, dads, brothers, sisters, and neighbors weight train because it is a safe fitness activity that helps them look better, feel better, and play better.

As popular as weight training is for adults, however, its value as a fitness activity for children has only recently been acknowledged, and that's because the notion of weight training for children was shrouded in untruths. These ideas had no

basis in scientific fact but were nonetheless powerful psychological deterrents preventing children, parents, and coaches from seeing weight training in the same light as Little League or ballet classes.

The question asked most often during any discussion of children and weight training is, can weight training be both safe and effective for children and adolescents?

The answer? A resounding yes!

Weight training produces the same array of benefits for young people that it does for millions of adults: They look better, feel better, and play better. More precisely, their balance between fat and lean body mass improves; their power, speed, and muscular endurance increase; their flexibility improves; and their bones and connective tissue become stronger.

The rewards of weight training are

not only physical, but also psychological. The rise in self-esteem that comes from lifting a heavier weight than you could last month or sculpting the body you want can only improve your confidence. Through weight training, shy, skinny, or overweight boys and girls can reshape their minds as well as bodies.

That's an impressive list of benefits! But you're not expected to believe them on blind faith. Topic by topic, this book will substantiate those claims by referring to the latest scientific research.

Let's begin our exploration of weight training for young people with the questions foremost in your mind, that is, the big questions.

Is weight training physically safe for young people?

Weight training is definitely physically safe, even for children as young as eight years old. Statistically, young people suffer musculoskeletal injuries far less frequently while participating in weight training than during more traditional sports activities such as basketball, soccer, running, football, wrestling, and gymnastics.

A respected pioneer in sports medicine, Dr. Gabe Mirken reports that "recent studies show that there is no evidence whatever that children are at increased risk of becoming injured from properly performed weight training."

In fact, weight training has actually been acclaimed as a positive way to prevent injury. A series of studies conducted in 1979, and thereafter repeatedly confirmed, demonstrates that the symptoms

of tennis elbow and tennis shoulder were less severe or were prevented entirely when the subjects incorporated a weight training program into their workout as preventive medicine.

Of course, some people have been injured while working out with weights, but there is nothing inherently dangerous about weight training. Carelessness, horseplay, improper technique, faulty equipment, inadequate warm-up, or poorly designed training routines—the usual causes of injury during any sports activity—are the culprits.

Everyone needs qualified direction while learning the basics of weight training. This is only common sense. Beginners, whether young or old, reduce their potential for injury when guided by an experienced supervisor.

This book was written with safety in mind. General safety procedures as well as pointers for specific exercises are emphasized throughout the program—even repeated when necessary. You don't have to be a worrywart, but you should follow the safety tips judiciously. Once you do that, you can fully enjoy your weight training and relish your improvements.

Is weight training psychologically safe?

Almost all kids worry about being too fat or too skinny, too tall or too short, too awkward or not athletic enough. It's no secret that physical appearance and athletic prowess are major factors in determining whether kids feel good or bad about themselves. In fact, studies indicate that a primary cause of depression among adolescents is dissatisfaction with their personal appearance.

This preoccupation with looks heightens when children are in late elementary and middle school—when the adolescent body is developing. At this time, the self-image also undergoes extensive changes, and many young people head for gymnasiums seeking to achieve a self-satisfying and peer-satisfying body. But is it all a waste of time?

Weight training changes the physical appearance. That's a fact. Physical appearance is vital to how young people view themselves. That's another fact. Moreover, there is a proven correlation between weight training and improved self-image. Clearly, a weight training program can boost self-esteem.

Contrary to popular belief, these positive changes are not limited to males and extensive muscle building. After reviewing a decade of studies, Jean Barrett Holloway and Thomas R. Baechle wrote in *Sports Medicine* that "participation in weight training can result in positive changes in self-concept and self-esteem for women of varying ages and abilities."

Weight training also offers physical achievement and its accompanying psychological benefits to boys and girls who are unable to excel in more traditional team sports. Children sometimes develop a lifelong sense of physical inadequacy and inferiority when unable to succeed in sports.

In weight training, however, success and improvement are measured on a personal scale and timeline. Every extra pound lifted is a reward, and the rewards continually accumulate during regular weight training. These personal achievements can become the foundation for lifelong confidence and self-esteem. In weight training, there is no peer pressure, no external opponent; there is no fumbled ball or missed shot, no benching or team cuts to dwell upon as one of adolescence's major crises. Whether you're tall or short, fat or thin, you are never the wrong size for weight lifting, and winning is what you do every time you step into a gym. What a lesson about personal accomplishment to give a young person!

Weight training is more than psychologically safe, it's an emotional booster shot, giving an extra dose of self-esteem right when it's needed most. Weight training can metamorphose a weak self-image into a strong one, and a person's self-image in youth often lasts a long, long time.

Will weight training stunt growth?

Contrary to what you might have heard, weight training does not stunt a child's growth. Let's expose that false notion to facts so that the next time you hear it, you can set the record straight.

Study after study has confirmed that weight training in childhood does not decrease the child's growth rate. For example, a study by Rians published in *The American Journal of Sports Medicine* found that weight training does not "adversely affect growth, development, flexibility or motor performance." Another, by B. Jacobson and F. Kullins published in *The Journal of Orthopaedic and Sports Physi-*

cal Therapy, concluded that "no damage to bone, epiphyses, growth tissue, or muscle" resulted from weight training.

But wait, there's something more. An unexpected discovery came to light in several recent studies that compared the growth rate of weight trainers with that of non–weight trainers—all of whom were about nine years old. The studies found that the weight trainers actually had an accelerated growth: Groups of males and females who weight trained grew faster than their nontraining peers. Of course, follow-up studies are necessary to determine the significance of the findings, but this information is intriguing to say the least.

Not one example can be found in the medical and scientific literature to support the idea that weight training stunts a child's growth. On the contrary, numerous meticulously monitored, fact-based studies conclude that a sensibly designed, supervised program of weight training is safe, and possibly beneficial, for a child's physical growth.

The evidence speaks for itself.

Will weight training damage bones and tendons?

Weight training will not deform the bones and tendons of growing children. During the past century, the popular literature on physical education linked bone damage to weight training. Thereafter, this mistaken belief permeated the culture, and coaches, educators, and parents did not question its validity.

Let's fight that myth with facts. It's

common knowledge that the stress of physical activity is necessary to build and maintain a strong, healthy muscular system. Think about how weak and limp muscles become after several weeks of immobilization in a plaster cast and you'll quickly realize how important physical activity is to maintain toned muscles.

Like muscle, bone atrophies when it is deprived of the stresses of normal physical activity. An atrophied bone is less dense—thinner in cross section. A thinner, less dense bone is a structurally weaker bone and is more likely to be injured during physical activity.

The stress of exercise increases the strength of bones. According to studies by

critical—as are self-responsibility and co-ordination. One child might be ready to begin a weight training program at five; another might not be ready at ten.

Children in the fourth, fifth, and sixth grades characteristically develop an interest in sports. It manifests as an intense desire to excel, a strong competitive urge, and a desire to improve specific skills. Individuals from this age group are able to learn detailed techniques and adhere to expressed safety precautions. For the right individual, it's an excellent time to begin weight training.

Two general indicators can signal a child's readiness to weight train. First, and most important, is the child's expressed desire to take part in the program. Second, as assessed by the parent or coach, is the child's ability to follow directions during participation. If either of these elements is absent, the child is not ready. Lack of desire or an inability to follow directions will hurt performance and endanger the child's safety.

Children younger than eight often express an interest in weight training, particularly if they see an older sibling enjoying it. However, children of this age are usually better suited for programs of resistance training, which use the body as the weight. These programs include exercises such as sit-ups and assisted pull-ups. Chapter 12 contains a program for children in this age group.

Most of the primary programs described in this book are designed for boys and girls roughly between the ages of eight and sixteen. But there are no rigid guidelines about age: emotional and intellectual readiness are the final determining factor.

How heavy is too heavy?

Any weight that prevents the person from performing at least eight repetitions without shaking is too heavy! The eight-repetition rule is a conservative one, developed for utmost safety. By following this rule, young people will stay within a safety zone on each repetition.

Relatively light weights are safer than heavy ones for two reasons. First, you can control a lighter weight more easily throughout an exercise movement. Second, lifting maximal weights might, according to some, harm the young person's still-developing musculoskeletal system. Although this is an unsubstantiated fear, until it is either confirmed or rejected by research, the prudent person will avoid maximal lifts.

Does the eight-repetition rule interfere with your progress? No. You reap all the benefits of weight training while minimizing the possibility of injury. This book definitely subscribes to the eight-repetition rule. It is a safe foundation on which to build a program of weight training. It makes both common and scientific sense.

Discipline yourself. Be safe, not sorry.

Chris's Corner

If your parents aren't sure about the safety of weight training, have them read this whole chapter and you should get the thumbs up!

How strong can a young person get?

How strong will you get? For the most part, the answer depends on how hard you work at it. Anyone can increase strength through weight training. The only requirements are effort and the discipline to stick to a regimen.

How fast will your strength increase? Credible studies report increases as great as 50 percent from a twenty-week training program. A 50-percent gain means that if you lift 100 pounds at the beginning of the program, you can lift 150 pounds twenty weeks later.

Some observers estimate even higher gains over a longer period of time. As Dr. Mirken reports, "Recent studies show that a properly supervised weight training program can double a child's strength in less than a year." Over the years, a person can continue to gain power by following the program. Of course, developing raw strength is only part of the benefit. The added power means a young person can swing a bat faster, throw a ball farther, or just revel in an ever-increasing strength.

Will weight training decrease speed?

As recently as the 1950s, the majority of coaches from all athletic activities were convinced that lifting weights would slow down their athletes. Even in the 1980s, a sizable minority of coaches discouraged their athletes from weight training for the same mistaken reason. Like many other false notions concerning weight training, the truth is quite the opposite.

A position statement by the American Academy of Pediatrics asserts that the increased strength acquired through weight training actually increases speed. Numerous follow-up studies support the same conclusion.

How does weight training make you faster? It increases the strength of muscle fibers—a correlation that numerous studies have confirmed. Stronger muscle fibers contract more quickly.

In practical application, therefore, the combined effect of millions of stronger muscle fibers increases the speed at which that part of the body moves through a given athletic movement. A stronger arm, leg, or torso is a faster arm, leg, or torso. That's why the present-day sports community embraces weight training as an important training tool for enhancing athletic performance. The experience of a broad spectrum of athletes, from boxers like Evander Holyfield to baseball players like José Canseco, has shown that weight training increases the speed of movement throughout all types of athletic events.

The athlete who doesn't weight train is at a competitive disadvantage, just as athletes from the 1950s would be if they competed against today's bigger, stronger, faster athletes—who do weight training.

The evidence is clear: Weight training increases speed.

Will weight training impede flexibility?

According to a study headed by Dr. Clark Rians, weight training has no adverse effect on the flexibility of a group of prepubescent males. Other studies, monitoring males and females of all age groups, reached the same conclusion: Lifting weights does not impede flexibility, even when the activity is taken to an extreme. In fact, in a study comparing different types of athletes, Jensen found that Olympic weight lifters were second only to competitive gymnasts in overall flexibility.

The range of motion of a joint—its flexibility—can actually be improved by weight training. That fact was published first in 1956 and has been confirmed many times since.

Weight training increases flexibility by lengthening a muscle's functional range, thereby increasing the joint's range of motion. Training to improve flexibility is particularly important for pubescent children. During the growth spurt, when the skeleton grows faster than the soft-tissue

muscles and ligaments, muscles and tendons tend to become tight. This discrepancy in development between the bones and soft tissue reduces flexibility and increases the potential for injury.

Can weight training help prevent injury?

Weight training increases power and flexibility, making muscles stronger and joints more flexible. This builds resistance to the sprains and strains that result from play or organized athletic activity. Underlying soft tissue is vulnerable to the collisions encountered during contact sports. The extreme example is a boxer with a flabby stomach who takes a solid punch to the soft midsection. Firmer muscles would lessen the pain. That's why for a hundred years boxers' training schedules have included sit-ups. Just look at Rocky Balboa!

Strong muscles help absorb the shock of landings or running that otherwise can be devastating to the feet, ankles, knees, and hips. That's one reason weight training has become an integral part of sports as varied as basketball and long-distance running. Weight training truly acts as preventive medicine by strengthening muscles and increasing flexibility.

Is weight training a total fitness program?

As wonderful as weight training is, it can't provide everything your body needs. Total fitness includes strength, muscular endurance, flexibility, and cardiovascular endurance. Weight training is the best form of exercise to develop strength and muscular endurance; properly performed, it improves flexibility. But weight training does not substantially improve cardiovascular fitness.

Aerobic exercises such as running, fast dancing, and swimming laps help improve cardicovascular fitness. Suitable alternatives include stationary bicycles, rowing machines, and stair climbers. But the exercise must be constant; just playing does not offer enough continued aerobic stress to develop and maintain cardiovascular fitness. That would be about as useful as a so-called power-building program of carrying out the garbage once a week.

Most experts recommend an aerobic activity that maintains what is called a *training heart rate* for fifteen continuous minutes per workout, three times a week. Although the training rate varies somewhat depending on age and health, the average healthy child between the ages of eight and sixteen is expected to maintain a training rate from 150 to 175 beats per minute.

Flexibility is another component of total fitness. Although weight training improves flexibility, many authorities recommend additional exercises. A series of slow, nonballistic stretches is best; the examples in chapter 9 will complement your weight training.

The components of total fitness—muscular endurance, strength, flexibility, and cardiovascular endurance—can be combined in a single workout. Stretch as part of your warm-up, follow with weight training for strength and muscular fitness, add fifteen minutes of a selected aerobic activity, and conclude with cool-down stretches.

The entire sequence will take less than an hour, three times each week. For your investment, the rewards are improved health, performance in sports, and self-esteem.

Can children use the same equipment as adults?

Only if it fits! That's why free weights, such as barbells and dumbbells, are recommended in this book. They can be used safely by people of all sizes and shapes.

Most popular exercise machines in commercial gyms aren't made for small bodies. They were designed to accommodate the average-size adult. Placing a small body into an adult-size exercise machine can be ineffective—even dangerous.

Imagine the difficulty a child would have driving an automobile. Although the driver's seat is adjustable, it's still impossible for the youngster to reach the pedals, see over the dash, and steer—all at the same time. Don't assume that it would be any more effective or safer for a child to use an exercise machine that was designed for adults.

Exercise machines can sometimes be altered to accommodate a child's body, perhaps by adding a pad here or a platform there. But modifying machines to conform to a special body size is dangerous unless you're an expert on body mechanics. Ten degrees added or subtracted from the machine's intended range of motion might place too much stress on young muscles and joints.

Although weights readily accommodate different body sizes, the safety of

these devices can't be taken for granted. Bench widths, hand-grip spacings, and seemingly innocuous things such as plate diameters and the length of a dumbbell handle must be selected to fit the user's body.

That concludes the general questions raised most often by parents, coaches, and young weight trainers as the child embarks on a program of weight training.

As you continue to read through this book, you will find questions and corresponding answers on more specific topics. So read on. All of your questions should be

answered by the time you reach the exercise programs.

Chris's Corner

After reading this, you're probably as excited about weight training as I was. I wanted to get to the gym right away. But don't start in on the exercises before reading more, or else your first trip to the gym may be exciting for the wrong reasons! There's more stuff to learn before you can train safely.

Chapter 2

How Weight Training Affects the Prepubescent Body

A weight training program is fundamentally the same for everyone—big or little, male or female, young or old. The results, however, depend partly on the age and sex of the participant. This is especially true for prepubescent children.

Prepubescent is a clinical term that describes a child's body before sexual maturity—before the surge of hormones that help create the stature and physique of the average adult. Prepubescent boys and girls of the same age are usually of similar height and weight. They grow at about the same rate, and when exposed to the same physical activities, they perform at about the same level. Differences in growth rates, absolute size, and physical abilities don't manifest until the surge of hormones during puberty. On average, the body remains childlike—prepubescent—until eleven or twelve years of age.

How can prepubescence be identified?

An early sign of puberty in girls is breast development, which is precipitated by the increased production of female hormones. Hence, prepubescent girls exhibit no breast development. When boys reach puberty, the enlargement of the testicles comes with the accelerated production of male hormones. This is accompanied by the growth of body and facial hair.

Of course, these are generalities—the usual physical changes that indicate that the body has left the childhood stage of development and begun the journey to adulthood. If in doubt, ask your pediatrician.

Do prepubescent boys and girls respond differently to weight training?

Children of either sex enjoy the same results from weight training. When comparing groups of prepubescent boys with

15

groups of prepubescent girls, the average results are much the same because the musculature of boys and girls are similar during childhood. It isn't until puberty, when in most cases sex-specific changes in build and stature add proportionately more muscle to the male frame, that strength differences become apparent. These strength differences then remain throughout life.

But the graphic differences apparent in adulthood are not found when com-

paring the muscular potential and performance of prepubescent children. Of course, individual boys and girls differ genetically in the quantity and specific analysis of muscle fiber. Some are born with more fast-twitch muscle fibers, which are better suited for strength building. Individual results of a program in weight training will fall on each side of average. But when a program produces enormously different results, whether comparing two children of the same or opposite sex, indi-

vidual genetic or environmental components are usually the deciding factors.

All else being equal, gender is not a determining factor in how a girl or boy will respond to weight training.

Do children get stronger from weight training?

Both boys and girls get stronger when engaged in weight training—despite the popular misconception that children can't make substantial gains in strength before the onset of puberty. That belief is founded on the erroneous idea that high levels of circulating hormones are necessary before a gain in strength can be made. Since children do not have high levels of circulating hormones, they cannot, some people assume, gain strength through weight training.

But modern research discredits that myth. *The Physician and Sports Medicine* published a study in which an experimental group of prepubescent boys demonstrated a 42-percent strength increase after a nine-week training program. It has also been documented that among people who have never trained before, 10-percent initial increases in strength are easily obtained after only two weeks of weight training.

Moreover, gains in strength are reportedly the same for both sexes, according to a study that tested a group of eight-year-old boys and girls. Another study of girls and boys between the ages of six and thirteen, conducted on machines specifically designed for young people, demonstrated a 48-percent gain in strength after a six-

week training program. The gains also correlated with improved motor performance, as measured in the standing long jump and vertical jump.

Finally, a broad survey of literature published in *The Journal of Orthopaedic and Sports Physical Therapy* concluded that "recent investigations overwhelmingly support significant strength gains in prepubescents as a result of weight training."

Does weight training increase a child's muscle size?

Although children can easily become stronger from weight training, they have a hard time growing bigger muscles. Pound for pound and inch for inch, impressive strength gains aren't matched by impressive muscle growth.

That a child can double his strength while experiencing little, if any, measurable increase in muscle mass seems puzzling. It has long been assumed from studies on adults that increased strength requires a proportionate increase in muscle size. In other words, we tend to think that a stronger muscle produces a bigger muscle.

But studies of children don't find a correlation between increased strength and increased muscle size. Apparently, kids can get much stronger without getting much bigger.

If not a bigger muscle, what is the physiological mechanism that accounts for strength gains in children? In the benchmark work on the topic, D. G. Sale, in *Perspectives in Exercise Science and*

Sports Medicine, suggests that the primary underlying mechanism for gains of strength in children are neural adaptations stimulated by the activity of weight training.

Neural adaptations include increased connections between the nervous system and existing muscle fibers, a change of nerve pathways to activate muscle fibers, and refined coordination between the nerve's signal and the muscle's reaction. Taken together, it means that the so-called nerve switchboards in the brain and spinal cord learn to rearrange nerve signals in such a way that existing muscle fibers are more efficiently incorporated during a movement in weight lifting. The result is an increase in strength.

What does all this mean? Kids aren't going to look like miniature Schwarzeneggers from weight training—no matter how much they work out. Although some increase in muscle size results from a child's weight training, significant increases in muscle mass won't occur until puberty.

Will weight training in childhood affect the number of muscle fibers later in life?

As recently as the 1980s, physiologists who specialize in the study of muscles proposed that muscle cells do not increase in number after birth. Hence, it was thought that weight training wouldn't add a single muscle cell to the number you had when you were born—that muscle-cell count was genetically determined. Many people once believed that the huge muscles that resulted from weight training reflected the muscle cells that had been present at birth—much like blowing up a box of balloons: The uninflated balloons fit in a small box; when blown up, they fill the room.

More recent preliminary research, however, casts serious doubt on this theory. It

Chris's Corner

Don't be discouraged if you don't start getting bulky and buffed right away. It takes time to grow big muscles. But you will see almost immediate improvements in sports, speed, muscle tone, and most of all, strength. Keep at it.

even suggests that intensive weight training at an early age can stimulate growth of new muscle cells! In other words, the number of muscle cells present at birth can be increased through weight training.

The issue of muscle-cell count at birth evolved from the convergence of several investigations regarding the intricacies of growth hormone (GH). This is a naturally occurring hormone that regulates growth and development in each of us. It has long been known that if our bodies produce too little GH, we won't reach our full growth potential. Conversely, substantial over-production of GH produces the giants among us.

In 1984, Serono Laboratories published a finding that GH increases the number of muscle fibers in preadolescents and adolescents. That same year, a European journal reported that the blood level of GH rises as much as 260 percent above normal both during and immediately following an intense workout with weights. From these two studies it can be inferred that weight training increases the production of GH, which, in turn, stimulates the production of new muscle cells.

But what practical impact does this have on a child who trains with weights? If further studies substantiate the preliminary results, such kids will have more muscle cells later in life than they did at birth, and these additional muscle cells will provide a competitive advantage throughout the child's athletic life: more cells that can be channeled into a specific athletic movement. At least, they will allow the young person to grow bigger and stronger.

One thing is certain, weight training won't reduce the number of muscle cells.

Is weight training safe for prepubescent children?

This question was addressed in chapter 1, but the topic has been subject to so much misinformation in the past that I want to reiterate the correct answer, particularly for the parents of preadolescent children: The scientific studies referred to throughout this book overwhelmingly conclude that supervised weight training is safe for children. This conclusion is supported by the American Academy of Pediatrics and the National Strength and Conditioning Association—two organizations that represent the breadth of opinion on the subject.

Properly conducted weight training will not damage bones, inhibit growth, decrease flexibility, impede speed or reflexes, destroy coordination, or injure joints. On the contrary, weight training has been shown to increase muscle strength, strengthen bones, improve athletic performance, reduce the risk of injury, enhance speed, increase flexibility, improve blood-lipid profiles, reduce body-fat percentages, and improve self-esteem.

ried on the frame. Second, broader shoulders produce a mechanical advantage as muscles work through the shoulder joint.

The broader, more mechanically advantaged shoulders of the pubescent and adult male account for the fact that the greatest strength differences between the sexes can be found at the shoulders. For example, the average female's shoulder strength is about 55 percent that of a male's, whereas a female's lower body strength is about 75 percent that of her male counterpart. These strength differences become noticeable at the beginning of puberty.

Hence, the normal pubertal changes in skeletal structure have a large effect on comparative training results. More muscle and a mechanical advantage translate into greater absolute strength gains for the young man than for the young woman. But that does not mean that young women should avoid training their shoulders. If anything, some young women might want to supplement their workout with exercises to strengthen the upper body.

Hence the same exercises are recommended for females as for males. Although the male will achieve greater absolute strength gains, there will be little, if any, difference in the percentage increase of strength when comparing a male and female on a similar program.

How does the male's increase in muscle mass affect weight training?

Larger muscles go hand-in-hand with a greater capacity for strength. Therefore, the male's natural increase in muscle size during puberty enhances the potential for greater strength. The issue, however, is purely one of size. As Jean Barrett Holloway and Thomas R. Baechle conclude in a review of the relevant literature, "unit for unit, female muscle tissue is similar in force output to male muscle tissue." Size is also a focus when comparing prepubescent males to pubescent males. The larger muscles of the pubescent males create a distinct potential advantage in absolute strength.

Muscle is muscle; whatever your sex or age, weight training increases strength. But because the pubescent and adult male have *more* muscle, the effects of weight training are correspondingly magnified.

What is the effect of hormones?

Hormone production is different for boys and girls during puberty. The boy's body begins producing large amounts of testosterone, the primary male sex steroid. It is testosterone that largely influences muscle growth in response to weight training. The girl's body, although containing some testosterone, does not produce it in large enough amounts to allow substantial gains in muscle mass.

Month after month and year after year, weight training causes the muscle-strength-muscle cycle to repeat: It is the driving force for males and females, adult or child. But testosterone is like a high-octane fuel that is naturally available to males—after the onset of puberty. Testosterone accounts for the male's natural increase of muscle mass during puberty and, combined with weight training, produces even bigger muscles. In turn, these bigger muscles create an even greater potential for absolute strength.

Should pubescent males take muscle-building drugs?

Some people might consider this a preposterous question. For others, it is foremost in their minds. A study released in 1990 by the federal government estimates that 262,000 students in grades seven through twelve have used steroids to enhance performance. The most commonly requested drugs are testosterone and growth hormone.

Stated bluntly, don't take steroids! Testosterone and growth hormone should not be prescribed or administered to children of normal stature. The human body is a highly complex system of interrelated chemical checks and balances. Ingesting synthetic hormones disrupts this balance—a delicate balance engineered over millions of years through genetic trial and error.

The consequences of tampering with the body, particularly regarding unnecessary hormone therapy, are not fully known. This is especially true during the developmental stages of prepuberty and puberty. An oversupply of a particular hormone can destroy the subtle chemical balances that guide the child's body through these critical growth periods.

In the short run, taking steroids during adolescence can turn off the body's normal mechanism for long-bone growth. That actually stops growth, causing the youth's height to stop short of its genetic potential. In the long run, extensive use of

steroids has been linked to hair loss, liver cancer, personality disorders, strokes, and heart attacks.

There is a place in pediatric medicine for hormone therapy—when symptoms justify interfering with the body's natural hormonal response. But most steroids are purchased illegally, with little advice for use beyond gym gossip and a desire to find a shortcut to enhanced performance in sports.

Muscles will grow big and strong from weight training and adequate diet. The process is a little bit slower than it would be by using anabolic steroids, but it's legal and a whole lot safer.

Chris's Corner

It may be tempting to speed up your improvement, but steroids aren't the way to do it. Weight lifting is sort of like a game, and steroids are like cheating. If you cheat, you won't feel as good about yourself in the long run.

Do training programs differ for young women and men?

You might think that the differences between the sexes would mandate a different training program, or at least different poundages. Not at all. The exercises are the same for both men and women. The sets are the same. The repetitions are the same. The training programs are the same. Suggesting that women require special training programs is a form of male chauvinism.

A young woman's muscle is physiolog-

ically similar to that of a young man. Although there are differences in the size of muscle fiber and overall body mass, the quality of muscle is equal. On average, males have larger muscle fibers when measured in cross section. Males are also taller and heavier during and after puberty. Taken together, these differences provide the male with an advantageous base from which to build absolute strength. That's why most studies find the average pubescent and adult female about two-thirds as strong as their average male counterparts.

But regardless of initial muscle volume or the levels of strength they start off with, both sexes respond in similar fashion to weight training. In fact, studies conclusively state that women achieve equal or even greater percentage increases in strength than do men when both undergo an identical program of weight training.

As for their size difference, the average young woman will begin the program significantly weaker than an average young man. But again, this does not mean that young women need a different training program. Like a young man of similar size, she may have to select a lower starting weight, but the exercises and repetitions will be the same.

Considering the long-range results,

genetic inhibitors limit the amount of muscle and strength that a young woman can ultimately develop. That's part of being female. Still, women can safely and effectively train to build their strength and improve their health.

Can weight training harm the female reproductive system?

The stress of some athletic activities can influence the onset of puberty. For example, the intense, continuous stress of long-distance running can often delay the onset of puberty in girls until the age of fourteen or fifteen. The childlike bodies of many teenage gymnasts are graphic evidence of delayed puberty.

Although it would seem unhealthy, the delayed puberty resulting from intense competitive gymnastics and running may not be of significant concern. A symposium of the American Association for the Advancement of Science concluded that delayed puberty or irregular menstrual cycles are a natural adaptation to strenuous exercise. The irregularities and delays self-correct when the intense exercise is reduced or eliminated.

In contrast to some sports, however, weight training is not associated with delay in puberty—or disruption of the menstrual cycle after puberty. That is probably because weight training lacks the high-intensity, year-round training regimen necessary for success in competitive gymnastics or long-distance running.

Young women can weight train without fear that the natural course of development through puberty and adolescence will be postponed. Weight training isn't stressful enough to cause developmental or reproductive irregularities.

Throughout the studies, there is no evidence whatsoever that young women should train differently than young men, and there is overwhelming evidence that young women will earn many benefits by adhering to a good program. The goal of a stronger, fitter, more athletic body is within the reach of every young woman.

Do girls and young women grow stronger through weight training?

All muscle tissue adapts to the stress of weight training by getting stronger, and girls and young women show remarkable gains in strength through this activity. Regardless of what a brother or boyfriend might like a girl to think, developing great strength is not the exclusive domain of males. In fact, when males and females of similar size and body composition are compared, there is only a 2-percent overall difference in strength.

Why, then, can the average male lift a heavier weight than the average female? The primary reason is physical size. According to Wells and Plowman, the average male is 10 percent taller and 11 kilograms (about 29 pounds) heavier than the average female. Another factor is traditional cultural attitudes. Society is far more likely to encourage young boys than young girls to engage in strength-building games and athletic events.

Several minor differences, however, exist between the muscle tissue of males who do not train and that of females who do not train: The female's individual muscle fibers, for example, are smaller than the male's. But this might also be because the female had engaged in fewer muscle-building activities, sports, or games. Comparisons of nationally ranked male and female bodybuilders find no difference in the cross-sectional area of muscle fibers.

Will young women get big muscles from weight training?

As mentioned previously, testosterone is a necessary ingredient for growing large muscles. Because females have very little testosterone in their blood streams, females of any age experience only a limited change in muscle size as a result of weight training. However, muscle growth, although limited, does occur in females.

Recent studies indicate that intense training elevates the blood testosterone levels of females, and this elevated testosterone level might induce the observed muscle growth. Most research still reports that significant muscle growth in females is rare. Several studies even indicate that the female weight trainer is actually more likely to lose size in her lower body—the hips and thighs—while maintaining the same body weight.

Of course, the female body does take on a more toned feel and appearance through weight training; a result most people consider a positive benefit.

What happens when young women take steroids?

Testosterone is the primary reason adolescent and adult males have larger muscles than females: All else being equal, more testosterone means more muscle. Some female athletes have taken testosterone-based drugs to stimulate greater muscle growth and strength; and for some, it works. The unnaturally muscular bodies of some female bodybuilders attest to that fact. The effects of steroids on the individual, however, are unpredictable. One woman might gain 20 pounds of muscle in a few months; another might experience little change.

Undesirable consequences abound. Temporary side effects of added testosterone in the female body include fluid retention, decreased breast size, acne, and menstrual irregularities. The permanent side effects can include loss of scalp hair, deepening of the voice, dark facial hair, and excessive growth of hair. Creating an unnatural level of testosterone with steroid therapy shifts the female's body chemistry and physiology toward that of a male.

It makes more sense to stay within the boundaries established by nature. Play it safe; stay away from anabolic steroids.

You now have a basic understanding of the interrelationship between weight training and adolescence. Here's some food for thought by Dr. Dietmar Schmidtbleicher of the Sportscience Institute, Frankfurt University, on why it has taken so long for weight training to become a socially accepted activity for young people:

"Coaches don't really know at what age they can start children on weight training. So they wait for a very long time and normally start too late."

Chapter 4

Guidance and Camaraderie: Establishing a Positive Relationship Between Adults and Kids

Chris and I gain many benefits from weight training. Clearly, we're both stronger and in better physical condition than we were before we began the program. His basketball, football, and track have improved. My racquetball game is better. But no other benefit equals the feeling of camaraderie we experience by sharing our leisure-time workouts. We sweat together, hurt together, improve together, laugh together, and play together. We are building better bodies, but we are also building closer emotional ties.

These ties also run through the rest of our lives. Our communication has always been good, but the workouts have added a new dimension to our relationship. Fathers, mothers, and children who already take part in family outings such as camping, hunting, or hiking know what I'm talking about. The planned activity, whether fishing or weight training, provides opportunities for interaction that are often overlooked during the hectic pace of daily life.

The following topics are intended as ideas you might like to consider as you train together and build your relationship. Every emotional connection is different, even between parents and each of their children—as I know from having coached and trained with my three kids. I don't profess to have all the answers, but Chris and I want to share what training together has taught us.

What is the traditional parent-coach relationship?

Year after year, many parents volunteer as coaches with the hope of becoming closer to their children, only to end the season frustrated with the results. The parent-as-coach and the child are immersed in a highly competitive, stressful arena that overemphasizes winning. The pressures of fairly selecting players and positions are compounded when coaches must judge their own children. The kid can't come home to a soft shoulder to cry on, because that shoulder belongs to the same person who controls the bench.

While it's certainly not always the case, the competitive nature of organized sports can bring out the worst in a relationship between parent and child. Frequently, the kids feel they must excel to meet parental expectations, or parents silently imply that their expectations haven't been met. Too often, a parent unknowingly takes on the role of the screaming coach when the child really needs an understanding parent. The confused children do not know whether they're dealing with Dr. Jekyll or Mr. Hyde.

Despite good intentions, the traditional role of parent-as-coach often burdens the relationship with unnecessary stress.

How does the parent-as-partner differ from the parent-as-coach?

Unlike the traditional coaches' milieu, the arena for weight training is a psychologically stress-free environment. There is no audience to please. There are no teammates' parents to appease. No opponents to conquer. No score. No winning or losing. No benching or choosing. Nothing to hinder the development of a positive relationship between parent and child.

As a result, the parent becomes a training partner who shares the experience, rather than a coach whose authority is absolute. The child still works toward physical accomplishment, but the timeline is flexible. Progress is not dictated by the length of the season or by quarters or innings. Weight training is an enjoyable family activity, not a test. All concerned feel better about themselves, and therefore about each other.

Unlike the traditional parent-as-a-coach relationship, a program for building strength through weight training is but the vehicle for communication between parent and child. The partnership is one-on-one. The relationship is one-to-one. Each relies on the other for support, motivation, and companionship.

How can we build communication?

Weight training is no different from helping a child learn mathematics, reading, or woodworking. The following are some guidelines on basic communication between the parent-partner and the child.

1. Train with your child; be a true partner.
2. Do your best to create an enjoyable environment.
3. Use verbal rewards to reinforce your child's improved skills.
4. Kids learn best by following a role model. If you live a healthy, active lifestyle, you will pass that legacy on to the next generation.
5. Don't push too hard or too fast. Respect your children for knowing their limits. Stop the moment an exercise hurts.

6. Assist your child as a spotter. Have your child assist you when it can be done safely.

7. Telling isn't teaching; your child learns by doing. Don't burden the child with too many instructions at one time.

8. Recognize even a partial improvement in form. Praise effort.

9. Help your child to set realistic goals that are consistent with the training program objectives.

Are there special considerations when training with daughters?

In 1990, *Sports Medicine* reported that our "children are encultured to view strength as masculine, an outlook which has depressed the pursuit and performance of strength activities by women." In other words, our daughters are taught to be so-called little girls. They are encouraged to assume stereotypical behavior including acting frail and vulnerable as a way of gaining approval.

Yet a female's ability is quite different from this cultural stereotype. Studies repeatedly conclude that the capacity to endure cardiovascular stress is remarkably similar between males and females. Researchers also conclude that male and female muscle tissue is similar in force output. Enlightened fathers and mothers must guide their daughters through the maze of cultural expectations.

How can parents help a daughter who weight trains? First, the parents must recognize for themselves that weight training is physically safe. Second, they must understand that the cultural forces perpetuating sexual inequality are remnants of the past. Third, parents must remember that the discipline and efforts made in a program of weight training are valuable experiences for their daughters; studies have proven that they can improve self-image and boost self-esteem.

Your daughter is just like any other training partner. Equal treatment is the appropriate treatment.

When and how should we design our own program?

Beginners should avoid designing individual programs until they have at least a year's experience. Chapter 10 lists the nine exercises comprising the free weights workout. Combined, they exercise each of the major muscle groups—a workout for the entire body. Working each muscle group according to this program serves as a solid foundation. After a year, the child's relative strengths and weaknesses can be more accurately assessed, providing the basis for a customized program.

With few exceptions, a balanced program in weight training for the full body is best for the kid who wants an enhanced sports performance. The thrust of the shot put, for example, begins in the toes and ends at the fingertips, with the force carried through the legs, hips, torso, shoulder, and arm. Any weak link in the chain of force detracts from the overall effort. It's the same when you throw a football. The rotational momentum of the rotating hips, driven by the thighs, is carried through the torso and translates into the linear momentum propelling the ball as it leaves the hand. All of this occurs in a split second of coordinated muscular action.

If and when it comes time to design an individual program, the parent or coach should guide the child toward retaining a full-body program. Certain body parts can be emphasized, but not to the point of upsetting the overall balance. The primary reason for focusing on certain body parts is to bring those areas up to the level of the rest of the body—not to ruin the physical balance by overdeveloping.

Remember a final, critical point if you consider modifying the free weights workout: Adult programs and their intensity of training must not be imposed on children. It's easy to expect too much from children, particularly if they are big kids, but regardless of size, a developing body must not be subjected to the physical stresses designed for adults. This means no maximal weights, no forced repetitions, and only limited sets.

Should we cut down on training during participation in seasonal sports?

It may seem unlikely at times, but there is a limit to a kid's energy. The trouble is, sometimes the child doesn't know it until there's a fall-off in academic or athletic performance. Balancing school, sports, chores, hobbies, weight training, and even psychological adjustments to physical growth, is often too big a load. Motivation and dedication wane, and the potential for injury increases.

During the seasons of competitive sports, encourage your child to reduce the intensity and frequency of workouts. Cut the training program to two workouts per week. Encourage reduction in sets and repetitions. Discourage increases in poundage.

Missing a few workouts in a lifetime of weight training won't interfere with reaching long-term goals, but this perspective is an adult sort of wisdom and often eludes a child. Parental guidance must be carefully but firmly exercised.

Are we helping our child develop a healthy lifestyle?

All parents want their children to grow up to be happy, healthy adults. Becoming a partner with your child in an exercise program certainly helps them, particularly since it's easier to establish patterns for a positive lifestyle at a young age.

The media has presented a strong case that the current generation of children are fitness wrecks; unfortunately, studies support the media's conclusion: Two out of every three children can't do a single chin-up. Nearly half of all boys can't touch their toes, and nearly a third of children are obese. With that in mind, doesn't it make sense to encourage your child to buck the trend? Fitness can begin at home, and you can be an active partner in an exercise plan that will reap rewards for every family member.

A concerned parent watches carefully over a child's education. It's just as important to take charge of your child's present and future health and fitness. The best way to encourage children to exercise regularly is to work out yourself. Along the way, the struggle of reaching for a common goal can make you closer to each other than you've ever been.

Part Two

As You Start

Chapter 5

Basics

Let's have a common language. Whether it's road signs on a highway or culinary terms in a recipe, a mutual understanding of descriptive terminology makes communication easier.

In the same way, learning the basic terms and concepts of weight training will enable you to communicate about it accurately. Soon the words will become second nature to you, and you'll be able to talk with a training partner, a coach, or a child more quickly and without fear of miscommunication.

What is resistance training?

Resistance training is any exercise in which some form of resistance, such as weights, makes movement more difficult. Weight training isn't the only form of resistance training, which includes many ac-

tivities, such as running up a flight of stairs or pushing against an immovable object (isometrics). This book, of course, focuses on weight training, particularly with the use of free weights.

What are free weights?

Free weights are barbells and dumbbells. They are not the Nautilus, Universal, or other machines that are found in professional gyms and health clubs.

Free weights are emphasized in this book for two reasons. First, free weights are the cheapest and most common weight training devices in the marketplace. A beginning set of free weights costs about fifty dollars (less than a pair of trendy shoes) and are available at most department and sporting-goods stores. That's a small investment considering the thousands of exercise hours they provide the whole family.

Second, free weights adapt to any body size. Many of the popular machines for weight training are designed to fit the average range of adult body sizes, but they usually don't fit a child's body—and improper fitting to a machine can be unsafe. This is not to imply that all machines are bad for all children, but you won't have to worry about the fit of free weights. They can be safely used by anybody.

What is progressive resistance training?

Progressive resistance is the essence of most weight training programs, and the foundation of the programs presented throughout this book. The term refers to the idea that as you become stronger and better able to perform an exercise, you increase the weight of the barbell or dumbbell used for that exercise.

Note, however, that progressive resistance means increasing the poundage that is used for an exercise. It does not refer to increasing the number of repetitions. Read on, and the differences will become clear.

How does progressive resistance work?

Progressive resistance training is based on the well-accepted fact that the body adapts to physical stresses that are systematically increased over time.

Imagine, for example, that when you begin weight training, you stress your muscles by lifting 25 pounds above your head ten times without resting. Your muscles adapt to the stress by getting stronger, and soon the exercise becomes much easier than it was at first. You add five pounds to the weight and find you are able to lift 30 pounds above your head ten times. With this extra weight, the stress returns. However, your muscles again adapt, and soon it becomes easy to lift the 30 pounds above your head. Then 35 pounds. Then 40 pounds. Your muscles have adapted to the gradual increases in stress—the resistance of the heavier and heavier barbell. Of course, you will not always choose to increase the weights. You will eventually reach a point at which you are satisfied with your progress and want only to maintain the level of strength that you have achieved. But until you reach the point at which you are satisfied, your body will continue to adapt to the increased weights as long as you take it slowly and safely. That's one of the basic tenets of weight training: Muscles become stronger and better adapted for stress through progressive resistance training.

What are repetitions?

In weight training lingo, a repetition, or rep, is one complete exercise movement. One squat, one curl, one sit-up, or one push-up are all examples of one rep.

When performing the exercises in this book, credit yourself with one rep each time you perform and exercise without stopping to rest.

What are sets?

A set is a group of repetitions done without taking a rest break. The group might include six reps, eight reps, twenty-five reps, or any other number. But whatever the size of the group, the concept is the same: A set is a group of reps. Thus, if you do a dozen sit-ups without stopping, you have done twelve repetitions—and one set.

How many sets should I do?

Many people are confused about how to start an exercise program. Some beginners go overboard, inviting strain or even injury and making such an effort of training that they begin to dread their workouts. Others don't do enough; they have the right idea—starting slow—but they do so little that they are disappointed with their improvement and never work up the momentum to keep at the program.

A happy medium for beginners is to perform two sets for each exercise that is part of their program. The first set will contain fifteen repetitions and will act as a warm-up. The second set, consisting of eight to ten repetitions and performed with an appropriately heavier weight, is the power set. This set places greater demands on the muscles, forcing them to adapt to the greater load by increasing in strength. This set is where your muscles get their full workout.

How much rest time is needed between sets?

You must rest for two to four minutes between your first and second sets. This rest period allows your muscles to refill energy reserves depleted during the first set.

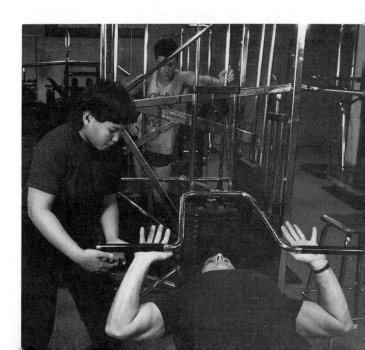

How much rest time is needed between exercises?

Rest periods between the different exercises, however, will vary for two reasons. First, your overall level of physical condition determines how soon you're able to move on to the next exercise. Depending upon how much exercise you're used to doing, you might be winded after a power set of leg lunges. Take a breather. You want to have a good workout, but the important thing is not to push yourself beyond what you can do safely.

Second, the length of the rest period depends on which muscle groups are worked by two successive exercises. For example, moving from a shoulder press to a tricep press might require a full two-to-four-minute rest period because both exercises use the triceps. Moving from the chest press to the leg lunge, however, would require no greater rest period than is required by switching from one weight station to the next, since each exercise works a different muscle group.

As always, there are exceptions to the rule: Although someone who has been weight training for months may be able to move from exercise to exercise, only stopping to catch her breath in between, a beginner might find an intense set of leg lunges so stressful to her overall system that moving on to the chest press would require a five-minute rest break before she continued her workout. There are no absolutes about rest periods. While a two-to-four-minute rest period between sets is typical for a beginner, it is not mandatory. The sequence of exercises and your level of conditioning will ultimately decide the length of rest required between sets and exercises.

How do I select a beginning weight?

Each person differs in strength, coordination, body weight, and body proportions. Exercise poundages also vary accordingly. For someone new to weight training, finding the correct weight for each exercise is no easy task. The first question in any new endeavor is where do I start? With weight training, the answer is found by experimentation.

Safety is the first rule of weight training, so if you are going to make a mistake in weight selection, by all means let it fall on the too-light side; it's a lot easier to just load a few extra pounds on the dumbbells next time than it is to suffer an injury that

has to heal before you can try again. Too heavy a weight in the beginning can also compromise correct form. It's best to begin with the lightest weight possible: the two-pound dumbbell bar without plates on the end, or the ten-pound barbell without plates. Gradually add weight over the first several weeks until you arrive at the proper poundage for the fifteen-repetition warm-up set and the eight-to-ten-repetition power set.

There's no need to be in a rush to use heavy weights. The workouts spent selecting the proper poundages for you are workouts well spent. Your goals for training must be long range to be safe and effective. So start your program on a solid foundation by following these guidelines and practicing correct form.

When and how much are weights increased?

When you are able to perform more than ten repetitions in your power set while using correct form, you can safely increase the weight at your next workout. Choose a new weight that exhausts your ability at eight to ten repetitions. A small increase in poundage is usually all that's necessary: perhaps a five- or ten-pound increase in the weight of the barbell, and half that much on each side if the exercise calls for dumbbells. Make sure the new weight can be lifted at least eight times during the power set.

Use this newly selected weight until ten repetitions once again becomes too easy. Then repeat the procedure of increasing the weight.

How can I retain flexibility?

Proper technique in weight training ensures that flexibility is maintained. First, perform each exercise through a full range of motion. For example, when performing curls, completely extend your elbow when working the biceps. Second, be sure to exercise the opposing muscle group. In the case of the biceps, the triceps is the opposing muscle group. Both the biceps and triceps act upon your elbow joint.

Perform each exercise through a full range of motion and exercise opposing muscle groups. This will ensure that your flexibility can do nothing but improve through weight training.

How can training partners help?

A young child must always have an adult training partner to teach and supervise safety. In fact, a training partner—who can be any age, shape, size, and sex—is a valuable part of anyone's workout. Mothers, fathers, kids, and friends can be great training partners for one another. They add inspiration to a workout, count reps, monitor form, and act as natural rest break by alternating exercises. Sometimes their toughest exercise of the day is dragging you into the gym on a day you're feeling too lazy to work out. In other words, training partners make training safer, more efficient, and more fun. Don't head for the gym without one.

What is a spotter?

A training partner acts as a spotter during many exercises. A spotter is a person who watches you go through your exercises, sometimes guiding the movement of the weights during or after an exercise. Most important, a spotter watches closely and will notice if a weight begins to slip from your grip or become too heavy for you to lift. For this reason, a training partner must be strong enough to safely lift a barbell off your chest when you're stuck. This is a perfect situation for a mom, dad, or older brother or sister to step in and actively support the young lifter's training efforts.

Throughout this book, special warnings are provided when spotters are neces-

sary for a particular exercise. Those warnings are incorporated into the exercise descriptions.

Chris's Corner

Training partners shouldn't be hard to find as soon as you show them this book. Working out is a lot more fun when you have someone to train with. It's also a great chance to team up with dad, mom, your brother or sister.

Must a child have supervision?

Training partners are often more than spotters or companions. They frequently act as supervisors, particularly if they're coaches, moms, or dads. Supervision is especially necessary if the weight trainer is a beginner, child, or adolescent.

The American Academy of Pediatrics recommends, as do the overwhelming majority of researchers, that trained adult supervision be present when children and adolescents engage in a strength-training program. It is also recommended that athletic coaches be trained in strength training. The National Strength and Conditioning Association offers home study with videotapes and written materials that are followed by a written examination.

Adult supervision supplements the limited knowledge and judgment expected of young people. In practice, that supplementation most often comes from parents and coaches. Regardless of source, it is important that supervision is provided for a beginning or young athlete.

This book is designed to provide a base of information from which an adult supervisor—mom, dad, or coach—can create a framework for supervision. It is offered with the stark realization that hundreds of thousands of young people are presently weight training with no supervision or available information source. But each young person is an individual, and each has a unique scheme of psychological and physical characteristics. At times, the adult supervisor must look beyond the information provided in this book to accurately assess the best interests of the individual child. Seek medical or professional consultations to determine the safety and efficacy of weight training for a particular child.

How often should beginners train?

Beginners, and those returning to training after a long absence from it, should train two times a week for the first three weeks. Use those three weeks as an introductory or reintroductory period in which you not only learn the correct exercise form and safety procedures, but select the proper poundages for your training program. Allow at least two days rest between training sessions during the introductory period; for example, train on Tuesdays and Fridays.

A workout schedule of two sessions per week permits your body to adapt slowly to the physical and psychological stresses of the routine, allowing your muscles, bones, joints, and mind ample time for recuperation.

After the introductory period, how much rest time is needed between workouts?

Both experienced weight trainers and over-eager beginners must never forget that time off between workouts is always necessary for muscles to grow in strength and size. The question becomes, how much time off is best?

The workouts recommended in this book for younger weight trainers will have the best results if you take a day off between sessions. For example, you might train on Monday, Wednesday, and Friday and rest the other four days of the week. If you're actively involved in a sport at the same time, it's okay to take two days off between workouts. The combined stress of sports and weight training often requires extra rest.

This is an important point that often surprises people. Although the stress of training is necessary to achieve an increase in size and strength, the actual gains do not occur during the workout. The rest day is the time when muscles adapt to the training stresses by synthesizing protein into additional muscle, increasing your strength and making minor repairs. Without this rest period, your body cannot make the very changes that you're training toward.

But too much rest can also hurt progress. Most researchers and weight training enthusiasts find that consistently resting more than two days without a workout or extensive exercise from sports is detrimental to the process of gaining strength and size. An extra day off during training or a short layoff when you're ill is nothing to worry about, but over the long run, sporadic training schedules ensure less-than-optimal results.

In a nutshell, intense workouts and adequate rest are indispensable partners promoting gains in strength and muscle. Rest at least one, and at most two, days between workouts, depending on your overall activity level. Three or more days of rest between workouts is too much.

Chapter 6

Setting Up a Home Gym

For children, it's often a home gym or nothing. Many professional gyms and health clubs, particularly in large metropolitan areas, practice age discrimination. Kids less than sixteen years old, and sometimes less than eighteen, with or without parental supervision, are barred from using the facilities because of management policy. That rule is usually established because a majority of club members, most of whom are in their twenties and thirties, don't want to share the training facility with children. Most management personnel won't do anything that offends a majority of paying customers.

But there are a number of advantages to working out at home. Home gyms offer convenience, maximum privacy, health enhancement, and a hub for family activity. The home gym also eliminates travel time to and from the gym, and no time is wasted waiting for another patron to finish using the equipment. In addition, a home gym can be economical when the onetime expense is compared to the accumulation of yearly dues at a health club.

So for a variety of reasons, Americans spend about 400 million dollars a year to equip home gyms with barbell sets, training benches, and multistation weight training machines. This chapter addresses questions regarding the wisdom of those purchases and what to do with the equipment once it's in your home.

Free weights or exercise machines?

Remember, free weights have two main advantages over machines: They accommodate any size body, and they are an inexpensive way to initiate a safe, effective program. Machines, however, have one advantage: They offer a stable position

47

that safely supports the child or adult during the exercise movement. On the negative side, most machines won't allow a full range of movement, thus inhibiting the development of coordination and flexibility.

Free weights offer unlimited exercise movements through a full range of movement for any body size. Besides this, free weights are virtually maintenance-free. Of course, they can't offer the stability of a machine, in which you strap yourself to the seat and push or pull precisely according to the machine's format. This drawback becomes an advantage, however, because free weights require greater attention to technique, more coordination, and more emphasis on perfecting a controlled movement, which are all goals of weight training itself.

Overall, free weights are your best bet for setting up that first home gym.

Can free weights be improvised?

It can sometimes be tempting to improvise weights to cut cost, with the idea that you will buy a real set of weights if you or the child sticks to a program. This is a mistake. Using household devices as so-called weights or filling plastic jugs with sand and water might seem an expedient thing to do, but in practice, the conglomeration of objects are hard to balance, nearly impossible to calibrate, and difficult to grip. All are unnecessary distractions to properly and safely learning and executing an exercise movement.

In addition, a messy jumble of old milk jugs doesn't give the average person much incentive to train, particularly in

that their appearance makes you want to keep them out of sight. You may find yourself, or your child, giving up after a short period of time, never realizing that the frustration of working with awkward substitutions for real equipment was the problem all along—not a lack of incentive.

Instead, treat yourself to a safe, inexpensive set of free weights and establish a serious tone to your regimen. You'll find that they are easier to handle, which lets you concentrate on the workout. Just looking at them can be an inspiration to train.

What free weights do we need to start?

Free weights come either in cast iron or as vinyl discs filled with sand or concrete. You will find the vinyl weights are short-lived, however, as they crack frequently and break during use. Also, the width of the vinyl weight puts a limit on the poundage that can fit on the bar. Conversely, a set of cast-iron weights can last a lifetime and offers nearly unlimited weight additions. It makes sense to start with a good cast-iron set.

Now that you've decided on cast-iron weights, your next question will be about poundage. Most sporting-goods stores offer a variety of cast-iron weight sets. If they don't have what you want in stock, they can quickly order it for you.

The best advice is to start with a 300-pound set. It will cost about one hundred dollars if you shop around. That poundage might be more weight than you need in the beginning, but it's only a matter of time before you'll need even more than that for some exercises.

The basic 300-pound set should include a five-foot or six-foot straight bar for barbell exercises and two short bars for dumbbell exercises. With the bars come an assortment of weighted plates and collars allowing you to adjust the weight of the bar. Additional plates can be purchased as needed at a later date. The ability to buy extra plates means that your first set will never become obsolete, no matter what level of expertise you reach.

For that very reason, select that first set of free weights carefully. Purchase a set that can be expanded when the time comes. Choosing a set that is quickly outgrown, or not adaptable to the needs of every family member, is neither cost effective nor conducive to motivated workouts. Employ the same depth of judgment in buying a weight set as you would in the selection of any major purchase. Remember that the right set can offer a lifetime of safe, effective use; the wrong one will end up as a useless dust collector.

What other equipment do we need?

In order to perform some of the recommended exercises you will need a weight bench. Benches are priced from thirty to three hundred dollars.

As with that initial selection of a set of free weights, choose that first bench with care. You want a bench that will do the job safely, and a higher price doesn't guarantee a better bench. Look for stability, strength, and adequate padding on the seat. A welded assembly is better than a bolted assembly, and higher-gauge materials offer more strength than do some of the flimsy assemblies that are on the market.

Don't buy a bench that looks like a toy. Chances are that it will be unable to withstand the continued stresses of weight training. Compromising on those initial pieces of equipment is a bad start on the long journey of an effective program in weight training.

Another necessary piece of equipment is a chin-up bar that can be placed in a doorway. You can buy one at the local sporting-goods store, or a more substantial homemade version can be constructed using a piece of heavy pipe and brackets. Whether purchased or homemade, install the bar carefully to ensure that it doesn't crash down during use.

Depending on the area of the house that you use as the training area, a protective floor pad might also be needed. Over time, workouts can destroy the finish of a hardwood floor, whereas the same workouts in the garage or basement can't do any damage.

That's all the equipment you'll need to start: free weights, a bench, a chin-up bar, and maybe a protective floor pad.

Can a multistation gym machine supplement free weights?

Machines offer a limited variety of exercises. More important, they are inappropriate for smaller bodies. Most machines are built for bodies from five feet, five inches to six feet tall. If you are outside that range, the safety and function of the exercise is somewhat compromised. Multistation machines can be used either as a supplement to free weights for family members who fit the machine, or for family members who want a quick workout within the parameters of the machine's limitations.

Do we need special shoes, clothing, gloves, and belts?

Another nice thing about exercising at home is that you don't have to worry if you're wearing this season's leotard. Comfort and function, not style, are what matter most.

The fitnesswear industry has boomed in the last decade, and workout clothes are available in all fabrics and sizes. So, if choosing colorful athletic wear makes you more enthusiastic about weight training, wear the brightest you can find. If you feel like making a statement about the great shape your body is in, tank tops and running tights may be the way to go to show off what you've accomplished. At home, you don't have to impress anyone but yourself, and loose sweats are just fine for weight training anywhere and anytime. One warning, though: Don't wear rubberized or plastic suits. They raise the body temperature unnecessarily by restricting evaporation from the body's surface.

Good gym shoes, however, are a wise investment. They should have a firm sole, arch support, and flexible top. They don't have to be expensive, but do not skimp where safety is concerned.

Gloves are a personal choice. They do help prevent calluses and make it easier for you to grip the bars. Fingerless gloves,

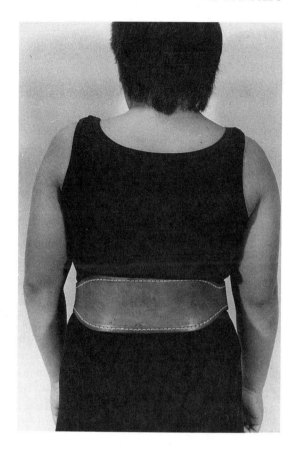

sweatbands, and wristbands, however, are accessories that are not essential to weight training.

Belts are another matter of personal choice. The premise behind using a belt is that it adds extra support to the lower back and abdomen while you perform exercise movements, particularly squats and overhead lifts. I've known many experienced weight trainers who recommend using a belt anytime that the machine or bench doesn't support the lower back. I've found no research to indicate that belts do, in fact, prevent injuries, but it's intuitively reasonable that the extra support adds a level of safety to the aforementioned exercises.

How can we shop smart for equipment?

Shopping for weight training equipment is a little like shopping for an automobile. Don't buy before you try.

Ask the salesperson for a demonstration of the equipment. If it's a bench or machine, ask about warranties. Check the reputation of the manufacturing company in case spare parts or repairs become necessary. Be sure to pay special attention to the padding and upholstery of the equipment. There's no need to ask for a warranty on a cast-iron barbell set; they're virtually indestructible.

If your bench or a machine requires home assembly, be sure to read the instructions before you leave the store. Take along a measuring tape to check that any large pieces of equipment will fit through your door before you bring them home.

Finally, look for bargains. You might find just what you need in the want ads or at a garage sale. But don't buy a set of weights, a bench, or a machine just because it's cheap. Be sure it's exactly what you want and need. It's hard to make a planter out of a weight stack.

Are mail-order exercise products worthwhile?

Magazine and TV adds often promote miraculous exercise contraptions that offer improvements in health and fitness through effortless exercise. As a general rule, stay away from those devices. If it sounds too good to be true, it probably is.

The benefits of exercise can only be brought about through the effort of exercise. The idea of no pain, no gain is at least metaphorically true. Although real physical pain is a sign to stop, you'll never make any progress without some sweat and effort. Using free weights or the equivalent exercise machine is a tried-and-true method of improving the tone, strength, size, and shape of muscles throughout the entire body, but you have to provide the work.

So, be a smart consumer. Examine every exercise device before making a commitment to purchase. Just because it's the latest, doesn't mean it's the greatest.

How much space do we need to weight train at home?

Every exercise recommended in this book can be performed within a six-by-eight-foot area. The required ceiling height depends on the height of the weight trainer, but anyone less than six feet two inches can get by within the height of the average room, even while executing overhead lifts.

A six-by-eight-foot area can accommodate a bench and a weight set—plus a spotter when needed. Of course, if you start out with a more sophisticated gym, or as you add equipment, more space will be required.

You do have room to set up your home gym. Exactly where depends on your living arrangements. If you don't have a spare room, or the corner of a basement or garage, consider the area at the end of the bed, on the patio, or in the family room. Storing the weights under the bed and pushing the bench against the wall after use is one alternative if you're really short on space.

A more serious approach requires a permanent space used exclusively for weight training and exercise. Each family must make this choice together in light of their particular situation.

How should we set up a home gym?

If the space is available, it makes sense to carefully design a permanent area for a home gym. A designated gym area contributes to your commitment, and that translates into a more serious workout.

Choose a well-lit, well-ventilated, temperature-controlled location that has a pleasing design. Make it a comfortable, inviting place to train. A dark, dingy, freezing basement or garage makes training a chore.

A mirror can be another important training tool, providing visual feedback on technique and form. The mirror also adds a sense of life when training alone and will make your gym look larger than it is.

Once you've decided on the location and equipment, use a trick that architects and interior designers use in laying out a space. Take a roll of masking tape and outline the places on the floor where you plan to place the equipment. This way you can easily determine if the anticipated arrangement is possible before you spend your hard-earned cash or drag a weight bench up a flight of stairs. Be sure there's

room for the family members who will use the gym to work out together safely at the same time.

A carpeted floor adds warmth to the home gym, but put down rubber throw mats where the weights will contact the floor in order to protect the carpet. If you choose an area that is not carpeted, be sure to purchase an exercise mat for sit-ups and stretches.

What the beginner needs

- A training partner as a spotter for safety and form
- Enough space to work: an area of at least six feet by eight feet
- A three-hundred-pound set of cast-iron free weights
- A weight training bench with uprights for holding a barbell
- A chin-up bar
- Gym clothing and gym shoes
- Enthusiasm!

Is weight training equipment all we need for a home gym?

For the strength and muscle-tone exercises, weight training equipment is all you need. A total fitness program, however, also includes cardiovascular exercise and training for flexibility.

For flexibility training you need only a mat on which to do exercises. A ballet barre along the wall is a useful addition, but not a necessity. The choice is up to you.

A variety of exercise devices offer cardiovascular fitness. More than adequate cardiovascular exercise can be achieved simply by running or walking around the neighborhood; of course, if you decide to train for cardiovascular fitness indoors, you will be able to train day or night and in any type of weather. Among the most common indoor exercise machines to get your heart pumping are exercycles, stair-stepping machines, rowers, and devices that simulate cross-country skiing. All work to elevate the user's heart rate.

A heavy punching bag offers another inexpensive and effective cardiovascular workout for males and females of all ages. Ten minutes of continually punching and kicking a heavy bag is an exhausting workout. Try it.

Why and how should we keep workout records?

Keep a clipboard in the home gym, with charts attached to plot your progress. This concrete proof of your development is a great motivational tool.

You can find record charts in the appendix. The first chart, the Workout Log, should be used to record each session. There's enough space on the chart to record at least a month's worth of workouts.

The second chart, the Monthly Progress Report, is used for recording long-term development. Enter the weight you're lifting for each exercise at the end of every month's training. At the end of six months, a year, and two years, you'll look back with amazement at the progress you've made. You'll know exactly where you would have been if you hadn't begun or continued your weight training program. I've personally witnessed the best of bodybuilders and weightlifters carrying their personal records with them year after year.

The third chart, Monthly Measurements, should be filled in at the same time that you're making your entries in the Monthly Progress Report. Monthly Measurements lets you keep a record of your growth rate and size changes. Many moms and dads have kept track of a child's height increases with marks on the kitchen wall. Now the whole family can extend that concept to include changes in the waist, chest, arms, and legs.

The home gym can be the hub for healthy family activity and interaction for many years to come. Take time and care as you plan and implement your workout area. You'll really appreciate it in the years to come. As Suzy Prudden, author of many exercise books, says: "Don't be frightened off from a home gym because you think you have to buy equipment you can't afford, don't need or won't use. You don't have to commit a lot of money or space; you just have to commit yourself."

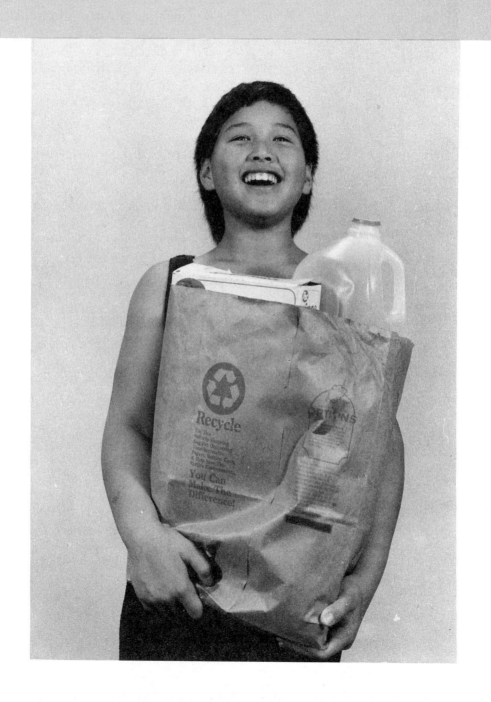

Chapter 7

Weight Training and Nutrition

The most important point that needs to be made about the nutritional demands of weight training is how ordinary they are. The rules of proper eating apply to people who weight train and people who don't; so, what and how much a weight trainer or non–weight trainer should eat is no more complicated than the well-balanced nutrition that should be part of any active young person's diet.

What diet is best when I'm weight training?

All bodies need a mix of proteins, fats, carbohydrates, minerals, vitamins, and water. But eating a well-balanced diet serves an especially important goal for the young weight trainer: It supplies the building blocks for the body's growth and maintenance. Depriving the body of any one of the nutrients adversely affects the results of your program because it can damage your general health.

A well-balanced diet is not a difficult goal to achieve. Follow the food selection plan suggested by the U.S. Department of Agriculture. The USDA plan (found in the Appendix) ensures that your diet will not slow down your progress in weight training.

Make a well-balanced diet a priority.

Should I eat more when weight training?

Exercise consumes energy. That energy, measured in calories, is provided by food. The more demanding the exercise, the more nutritious your food must be in order to replenish the energy reserves that are taxed during exercise.

You may be surprised to learn, however, that weight training is not a big energy consumer. An average weight trainer expends less than five-hundred calories during a workout. That's equivalent to the calories in a cheeseburger. The precise energy expenditure during a typical workout depends on which exercise you're doing; the poundages lifted; and your size, of course, but there's really nothing extraordinary about the energy demands of weight training.

Do weight trainers need extra protein?

A balanced diet supplies all the protein needs of young weight trainers. In other words, their bodies need nothing special; extra protein will not increase strength or muscle mass.

Chris's Corner

> *You may have heard that people have to pig out on high-calorie foods to gain muscle. That's false. The truth is, you have to eat a balanced diet and train hard. Have a combination of everyday foods like meat, fruits, vegetables, and milk.*

Old-time weight lifters and body builders assumed that eating enormous quantities of protein was necessary to build strength and muscle. Some ate as much as five pounds of beef each day—until their bodies responded with illnesses related to the unbalanced diet of too much meat.

The following is a safe general rule: ½ gram of protein per day for each pound of body weight. That means that a 100-pound weight trainer needs to consume about 50 grams of protein in each day's food. That much protein can be found in a chicken leg and two cups of milk.

Protein is a basic ingredient of any diet. That is because the muscles, brain, liver, and heart are mainly made of protein. But the average American's protein intake is more than enough to satisfy the body's needs. Gorging your body with extra protein doesn't help, and it *can* hurt.

How many meals a day are recommended?

Three meals a day are okay. Dividing the same food intake into five smaller meals throughout the day is better. At least that's what the studies indicate.

Five small meals provide a more stable supply of nutrients for the body's growth and maintenance activities. That's because the body can break down the nutrients and absorb them more efficiently with a larger stomach and intestinal surface area per unit volume of food.

With a more consistent intake of food, your day will proceed without the highs and lows of a fluctuating energy level. Inside, your body is able to carry on its sequence of growth and maintenance activities uninterrupted, because it isn't waiting for the next meal to provide crucial raw materials.

Of course, the more meals you eat through the course of a day, the smaller the individual meals have to be. Your total food volume should be the same whether eaten in three or five meals.

Are vitamin pills or protein supplements needed when weight training?

A well-balanced diet provides the vitamins, minerals, and quantities of protein necessary for general health and successful weight training.

As an insurance policy, a normal-dosage multivitamin and mineral tablet won't harm you. You should not, however, consume megadoses of any vitamin or mineral. High doses of fat-soluble vitamins such as A, D, E, and K can be retained in your body's tissue and produce toxic side effects. Besides, high doses won't improve your weight training performance.

Protein supplements, however, are absolutely not necessary for a normal child or young adult who eats a well-balanced diet. If you are ingesting less than the recommended amount of protein, don't resort to protein supplements to fill the gap. Just adjust your selection of foods appropriately.

Can weight training help me gain weight?

Working out with weights often increases body weight, because extra muscle developed through training increases the overall weight of the body. That's the reason that people who want to increase their body weight through weight training emphasize leg exercises; the legs and hips account for a majority of the body's muscle mass, so it makes sense to select exercises that can produce the greatest increase in muscle mass.

Weight training also increases body weight in another way. Like all exercise, weight training will, over the long term, induce the body to consume more food as fuel. But if the extra food delivers more calories than are burned during the exercise, extra body fat will form.

The best combination for the right type of weight gain is to emphasize leg training during your workout and to match the volume of food you eat to the number of calories you burn. That way, every ounce you gain will be muscle.

Should I weight train while on a weight-reduction diet?

The principles of any weight-reduction diet require consuming fewer calories than the body needs for growth, maintenance, and activity level. When you expend energy through exercise, and there is also a deficit in the energy being consumed through food, the body taps energy that has been stored within muscles and other organs. Essentially, the body feeds on itself when outside energy sources are unavailable. The body loses weight as this stored energy is burned for fuel.

A safe weight-reduction diet will lead the body to choose the right menu: To feed on excess fat rather than muscle, bone, or vital organs. Don't starve yourself. Although many children are overweight—and this is definitely unhealthy—a crash diet is not going to help them. A doctor can determine how many calories a child should ingest and may, in fact, recommend that a child who is growing taller merely maintain his present weight rather than try to lose pounds.

Weight training in combination with

dieting encourages the body to burn excess fat rather than muscles, bone, and organs. The reason is analogous to the old adage that the squeaky wheel gets the grease. The dieting body adapts to the stress of exercise by disproportionately replenishing the muscle being exercised (the squeaky wheel) with stored fat.

A practical example of the connection between diet and exercise can be explained by comparing two 140-pound dieters through the course of a diet. One weight trains, the other does not exercise.

Say that both lose 30 pounds; how do the two dieters differ? The weight trainer will have gained muscle and lost fat. The nonexerciser has actually lost muscle while retaining proportionately more fat. That's the reason dieters who abstain from exercise often look flabby at the conclusion of a diet.

As yet another bonus, weight training, like any exercise, is a short-term appetite suppressant that makes dieting less painful by vanquishing the craving for food between meals. If you can hold off snacking until your allotted training time, a trip to the gym is as filling as a trip to the refrigerator. Your hunger will seemingly miraculously disappear for several hours.

Include weight training as part of your diet package. You'll be healthier, and you'll look better.

Can I spot reduce with weight training?

Spot reducing is absolutely not possible through weight training. A thousand sit-ups a day for six months won't remove an inch of fat from your stomach. Those sit-ups will firm and tone the muscles of the stomach, but removing inches of fat requires dieting.

When dieting, no form of exercise can target specific areas of the body for weight reduction. As the body feeds on itself for energy supplies that aren't provided by food, it taps fat reserves found in all parts of the body. The fat loss is proportional. You'll lose a little bit from the front, a little bit from the back, a little bit from the top, and a little bit from the bottom.

However, weight training combined with diet will reshape your body by firming the body and eliminating fat. One without the other is only fighting half the battle. Together, weight training and proper nutrition can give you a trim, toned body of which you can be proud.

Take heart in the fact that weight training and diet combined will work. There aren't any shortcuts, but the results will be worth the wait.

Chapter 8

Training Safely

Working out with weights—an activity that not only increases strength and energy, but is also fun—could be one of the best things you ever do for yourself. The best way to reap all the benefits of training, though, is by lifting safely. With the right program you can avoid soreness and injuries, ease smoothly back into training after layoffs, and generally work out with consistency for as long as you wish.

What causes muscle soreness?

There are two types of muscle soreness, neither of which is a pleasant experience. The first, described as acute, occurs while you're actually engaging in a strenuous physical activity. It's that intensely painful, burning sensation that you experience in your legs when you're sprinting as fast and as far as you can. Fortunately, once you stop, the pain quickly subsides as you catch your breath and allow the bloodstream time to deliver oxygen to your overworked, oxygen-depleted muscles.

Delayed muscle soreness strikes from twelve to forty-eight hours after you exercise. It's the pain of overextending untrained muscles after a weekend of basketball or a Sunday afternoon of gardening. Although children seem to be constantly active, the extra demands of weight training can cause them to experience delayed muscle soreness.

Delayed muscle soreness is actually a manifestation of a minor injury: If we could look through our skin and examine those painfully sore arms and legs, we would find microscopic tears in the tissue of our muscles, ligaments, and tendons. Except in extreme cases, soreness is nothing to worry about. The pain will subside in a day or two as the body quickly heals itself.

How can I minimize delayed muscle soreness?

The occurrence and severity of delayed muscle soreness can be greatly reduced by following some sound training principles:

1. Make sure to include both a general and a specific warm-up as part of the weight training program. A warm-up program is suggested in chapter 9. The specific warm-up—a slow and steady set of fifteen reps—is particularly important, because it increases blood flow to the specific muscle group being exercised, preparing it for the stress of the intense power set that follows.
2. Control the exercise movement. Don't jerk, explode, or bounce the weight. Such sudden movements dramatically increase the pressure on muscles and joints.
3. Avoid negative or eccentric movements.
4. Don't be in a hurry to lift heavy weights. A young person, particularly, should spend the first several weeks of the training sessions gradually increasing poundages to find appropriate weights for the warm-up and power sets. The stress of going all-out during those first several workouts is sure to make a beginner plenty sore.
5. Cool down after the workout with the same stretches recommended for the warm-up. The cool-down is important! Don't neglect it.

How can I avoid injuries?

Injuries do happen while weight training. But more often than not, the injuries result from improper exercise technique, inadequate warm-up, or falling prey to the how-much-can-I-lift? syndrome. With beginners, there is also a higher correlation of injuries with overhead lifts.

Conversely, the best prescription for staying injury-free is an adequate warm-up, paying attention to and practicing proper exercise form, and gradually increasing poundages over a period of workouts until you've arrived at the proper poundages for your warm-up and power sets. And it bears repeating: Beginners should avoid standing overhead lifts.

An attentive, knowledgeable adult supervisor is commonsense preventive medicine for a child engaged in physical activity, whether it be on a playground, a baseball diamond, or in a family weight room. A parent or coach can supplement the judgment of a younger person, particularly when the activity is new to the kid.

Is it possible to overtrain?

Too much stress or not enough rest can lead to a physical or emotional depression. Weight trainers can overtrain by doing too many exercises or sets per body part or by training too frequently.

That's one reason this book recommends two sets of each exercise, two exercises for each body part, and three training sessions per week. The stress load of that schedule is tolerable for the average child or beginner. As the child matures or the beginner becomes better adapted to the stresses of a regular weight training schedule, the sets, exercises, and training frequency can be increased.

Why should beginners avoid overhead lifts?

Although injuries from weight training are infrequent, those that do occur, according to Dr. J. R. Ryan and Dr. G. G. Salciccioli, are most often the result of lifting a weight overhead from a standing position. More often than not, those injured are beginners.

It's easy to understand why. Standing while holding a heavy object at arm's length overhead requires simultaneous co-ordination, balance, strength, technique, and relaxation under stress. Beginners, simply because they are beginners, have difficulty integrating these necessary components into a synergistic whole.

This is not meant to put an absolute ban on overhead lifting. The bench press and chest fly, which are part of the beginner's workout, are technically overhead lifts, but the body is safely supported by a bench while the exercise is being performed. Holding a weight overhead while standing is the risk for people new to weight training.

Exercises such as standing overhead presses can be safely incorporated into the training routine after the young weight trainer has had ample time to adjust to the training arena.

Don't become a sorry statistic. Wait until you, or your child, are familiar with the nuances of weight training before adding overhead lifts to the training program.

How should I train after a layoff?

A layoff might come about for a number of reasons: a summer vacation, an injury, a conflicting activity, or even temporary boredom with training. Whatever the reason, approach the return to training cautiously.

Return from a layoff as if you were a beginner training for the first time, gradually building up the poundages and intensity of the exercises over a period of several weeks. Give your body time to reacclimate to the stress of weight training.

Jumping back into training at your prelayoff intensity is sure to overtax your muscles and tendons. It will cause extreme soreness for several subsequent workouts, and you could force yourself back into another layoff.

Avoid painful muscles and potential reinjury; take time before you return to your old form.

Chris's Corner

When people find out that you weight train, sometimes they wonder how much you can lift at your prime condition. The next section explains why lifting the heaviest weight possible isn't necessary to build super strength—and might even be dangerous.

Why not perform exercises with maximal weights?

Performing an exercise with the maximum number of pounds you can lift requires using a weight so heavy that you can lift it only once. Although research is inconclusive, weight training authorities recommend caution, stating that maximal lifts might increase the chance of structural injury to the young person's developing skeletal system.

As William Kraemer observed in an excellent paper written with several other experts in the field and published in *Pediatric Exercise Science*, "The load utilized in performing resistance exercise has been a primary point of concern. Some have feared that maximal or near-maximal lifting performed consistently during training could increase the probability of structural injury in children."

This doesn't mean that maximal lifts will cause structural damage. Research hasn't proven that to be the case. But a responsible recommendation is to avoid maximal lifts until the safety issue is conclusively resolved.

Maximum-weight lifts don't add to the value of a training session anyway. Studies have demonstrated that performing four to eight reps per set is best for developing strength; and even higher reps, more than twelve, are best for developing muscular endurance.

Avoid answering the question, how much can you lift? You have nothing to gain, and perhaps, something to lose.

Why not forced reps?

Forced reps, or assisted reps, are repetitions performed with a training partner's help. For example, if you could bench press 200 pounds on your own, you would use 210 pounds for a set of forced or assisted reps. During the forced rep, your partner would help you through the most difficult angle of the exercise—the sticking point. Hence, the exercise feels heavy throughout the motion.

Forced reps are a wonderfully effective training vehicle for adults, because each repetition is an all-out rep. You push to your limit with each repetition, whereas normal sets demand all-out muscular effort only during the last rep or two of a set. A set of forced reps produces more stress on the muscle, and your body responds by adapting to the heavier weight.

Prudence, however, again requires that maximal reps not be an ingredient of a young person's training program. Forced or assisted reps are, in reality, a set of maximal reps. Just because a training partner assists during the exercise doesn't diminish the stress on the young person's muscular and skeletal systems.

Why avoid cleans, jerks, and other explosive lifts?

A maxim of athletics is that a quick, explosive movement carries more risk of injury than a slow, methodical movement—and this holds true for weight training.

The explosive movements of weight training are the snatch, clean, and jerk, and correctly performing these lifts requires moving a heavy weight with great speed. The combination of speed and weight produces tremendous force, which manifests as tremendous muscular stress—sometimes too much stress for a developing body. As F. Allman has reported, the vast

Part Three

Time to Train

Chapter 9

Warming Up to Work Out

Okay, you've been patient long enough; now you're ready to actually get moving. But before you begin weight training itself, you'll want to ease your body into action, using a warm-up. It's tempting to skip the warm-up, but don't. It's a vital part of your workout—each and every time you exercise.

How does a warm-up benefit the body?

A warm-up does just what the word implies—warms the muscles that will be used in exercise. A warm-up routine prepares the body for the stress of weight training. As a result, the body responds with fewer injuries and fewer sore muscles and joints. If you forget to warm up, your muscles will feel tight as you lift, inviting a painful pull or tear when you command a movement that your body isn't ready for.

Again, you must warm up every time you work out. Remember that your body has more than five hundred muscles. Although the exercises in this book emphasize certain muscle groups, make no mistake that many of the remaining muscles play a supporting role in the exercise movement. The entire cast of performers should be warmed up and ready to go.

What's the best way to warm up?

An adequate warm-up has two parts: a general warm-up, which includes light aerobics and general stretching, and a warm-up set of lightweight, high-repetition lifting.

You should begin with the general, full-body warm-up. The general warm-up actually raises the body's temperature and increases the rate at which blood flows through your muscles.

69

The aerobic portion of the general warm-up should last from five to ten minutes. You might choose light jogging, fast walking, or peddling on a stationary bicycle while you watch TV. After the aerobics, perform a series of slow stretches. A good grouping of stretches is listed at the end of this chapter.

The second part of the warm-up is a low-weight, fifteen-rep set of the exercises you do in the free weights workout. This first light set prepares the muscles for the all-out effort of the power set that will follow it. Performing a lighter, less stressful version of the exercise you're about to engage in serves as a specific warm-up for the muscles used during the exercise.

WARM-UP STRETCHES

Shoulder Shrug

How to do it

1. Stand with feet placed shoulders-width apart.

2. Raise both shoulders upward toward the sides of your head.

3. Lower your shoulders, reaching both hands toward the floor. That's a rep. Do 15 reps, then shrug each shoulder by itself 15 times.

Hamstring Stretch

How to do it

1. Sit on the floor with both legs extended.

2. Slowly reach to your left ankle with your right hand, pausing 30 to 40 seconds in the stretched position.

3. Return to the starting position and slowly reach to the opposite side. That's a rep. Repeat the stretch 10 times.

Adductor Stretch

How to do it

1. Sit on the floor with your feet to-gether and your knees to the side.

2. Gently press your knees to your elbows. Hold this position for 30 to 40 seconds. That's one rep.

Thigh Stretch

How to do it

1. Sit on your left hip.

2. With your right hand, pull your right ankle toward your hip.

3. Hold this position for 10 to 15 seconds. Repeat with the opposite leg.

Side Bend

How to do it

1. Stand with your feet shoulders-width apart.

2. With your left elbow pointing toward the ceiling, move your left hand toward your left armpit. At the same time, reach toward your right ankle with your right hand.

3. When you've stretched as much as you comfortably can, slowly return to the upright position. That's a rep. Repeat the exercise on the opposite side.

Sky Stretch

How to do it

1. Stand with your feet flat.

2. Stretch your hand toward the sky, reaching as high as you can for 10 to 15 seconds.

3. Slowly relax and lower your arm. That's a rep. Repeat on the opposite side.

Calf Stretch

How to do it

1. Stand 3 to 4 feet from a wall or a training partner.

2. Lean forward and place your hands against the wall or against the hands of your partner. Stretch the calf of your rear leg, and hold the position for 30 to 45 seconds. Bend your knees if necessary to fully stretch the calves.

3. Return to the starting position and repeat with the opposite leg.

Chapter 10

The Free Weights Workout to Strengthen and Tone the Whole Body

After completing your general warm-up, you're ready to begin the training program. Remember, be careful as you select the poundages for your fifteen-rep warm-up set and your ten-rep power set. For the first several workouts, safety and form must be your overriding considerations. Don't try to see how much weight you can lift.

The free weights workout combines nine exercises, each of which is designed to strengthen and tone a particular part of your body. Complete the exercises in the numerical sequence, starting the workout with the lunge and completing the workout with the standing lateral raise. You'll find that following the suggested sequence contributes to an effective and efficient weight training workout.

Safety tips

1. Before using the weights, always check that the collars (the fasteners on dumbbells and barbells) are tightly fastened.

2. Have a spotter standing by, particularly when you are using weights heavier than usual. The spotter can check correct posture and be ready to catch the weight if you lose your grip.

3. Remember, the quality of the movements is more important than the quantity you move!

Ready? Here we go!

LEG EXERCISES

Lunge

Exercise emphasis
- thigh (front, rear, inside)
- hip
- lower back
- calf

Equipment Needed
- two dumbbells

Note: Don't use barbells for the lunges. Dumbbells are easier to balance and provide the necessary resistance.

WRONG WAY ☞

Beginners: Spend the first several workouts practicing correct form without using dumbbells. Once you're able to perform 10 perfect reps with each leg without the weight, then it's safe to add the dumbbells.

How to do it

1. Stand upright with your feet placed shoulders-width apart. Hold dumbbells at arm's length, your palms facing toward the thighs.

2. Keeping your head up and your back straight, take a long step forward with ei-

ther foot. Plant the foot and drop your hips until the lead thigh is parallel to the floor.

3. Push backward and upward with the lead foot.

4. Stand erect, going back to the starting position.

Take Care of Your Knees! The correct bend is 90 degrees. Do not allow too much knee bend.

WRONG WAY ☞

5. Repeat the exercise with the opposite leg. Alternate legs until you've completed 10 repetitions with each leg. That's one set.

Step-Up

Exercise emphasis
- thigh
- hip
- lower back

Equipment needed
- weight bench
- two dumbbells

Note: Don't Use Barbells. Dumbbells are easier to balance than barbells and are just as effective.

Caution: Check your exercise bench for stability before beginning this exercise.

Beginners: Practice the exercise without weights until you can do 2 sets of 10 perfect reps.

How to do it

1. With feet together, stand facing the *end* of a weight bench. Hold dumbbells at your sides.

2. Stepping up with your right foot, stand on top of the bench.

WRONG WAY ☞

3. Pause at the top.

4. Step down to the floor, starting with the left leg and following with the right.

Chris's Corner

The step-ups are hard, and they will burn very much if you do them right. You're going to feel like you're out of breath after step-ups, but don't get discouraged; it's the best exercise I've ever done for my legs. The form is important. Good luck!

5. Repeat the movement, stepping up with the left leg. Continue to alternate legs until you've completed 10 reps with each leg. That's a set.

BACK EXERCISES

Pull-Up

Exercise emphasis

- upper back (lats, or lateral muscles)
- chest
- back of shoulders
- biceps (front of arm)
- forearms

Equipment needed

- chin-up bar

Beginners: The pull-up is an essential exercise, but most kids can't do even one when they begin training. That's why spotter-assisted pull-ups are highlighted here. The spotter should be heavier than the trainer in order to provide stable resistance during the exercise.

2. Pushing against the spotter's hands only when absolutely necessary to complete the movement, pull your body upward until your chin is even with the bar.

3. While maintaining control, lower your body to the starting position. Be sure to use the spotter's assistance only as much as necessary as you lower your body.

Three ways to add resistance

Combination reps: When strong enough, perform the first several reps alone before using the spotter's assistance.

How to do it

1. Hang from the bar. Grip the bar overhand. Space hands shoulder-width apart on the bar. Feet are supported by the spotter's cupped hands.

Regular pull-ups: Use the weight of your entire body as the resistance.

Weighted pull-ups: Add resistance by strapping a weight around your waist after you are able to perform 10 regular reps without weight.

Note: Varying your grip will affect different muscles groups. Once you've perfected the basic pull-up, try a close grip, a wide grip, or a forward grip.

Chris's Corner

> *From this exercise, you'll get stronger arms, like a little Hulk Hogan. Make sure you have a spotter if you're a beginner. You'll need help getting started.*

Bent-Over Row

Exercise emphasis

- upper back
- back of shoulders
- biceps
- forearms

Equipment needed

- one dumbbell

It's best to use only one dumbbell for the bent-over rows. Bent-over rows that use barbells or two dumbbells increase the potential for injury, whereas if you place the knee and hand on a bench, it stabilizes and protects the upper back during the full range of motion.

Also, if you concentrate on the muscles of one side, you're able to get a fuller range of motion, working the lat muscles of the back and arm. Think of bent-over rows as the pull exercise—the opposite movement of the chest press, the push exercise.

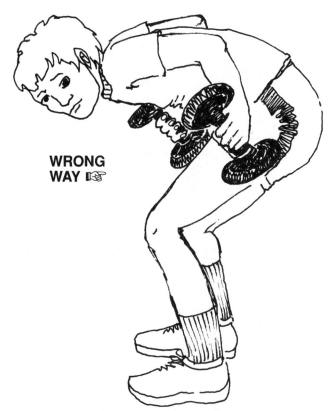

WRONG WAY ☞

WRONG WAY ☜

WRONG WAY ☜

How to do it

1. Place your left knee and left hand on the bench, positioning your back parallel to the floor. The dumbbell should hang from your right arm, stretching the back, shoulder, and arm toward the floor.

2. Pull the dumbbell upward, making sure to keep your elbow pointed toward the ceiling. Momentarily pause at the top.

Sit-Up

Exercise emphasis
- abdominals

Equipment needed
- slant board, for slant-board sit-ups
- one dumbbell, for advanced sit-ups only

Athletes need abdominal strength

During athletic movements, strong abdominals are needed to carry the force generated by the lower body into the upper body. If you don't want your stomach to look like the Pillsbury Doughboy's, begin doing these sit-ups!

Beginners: If sit-ups with hands clasped behind the head are too difficult, placing your hands on the stomach or behind the thighs will make them easier.

Special Notes: The legs are kept bent because straight-leg sit-ups place too much pressure on your lower back. Bent knees allow you to strengthen the abdominal muscles at the best angle. The sit-up must be a controlled motion. Don't jerk your

3. Lower the dumbbell toward the floor, maintaining control throughout the movement. Allow the dumbbell to stretch your back, shoulder, and arm. That's a rep. Now do 9 more!

4. After completing 10 reps with the right arm, switch positions on the bench and complete 10 reps with the left arm. Ten reps with each arm equals one set.

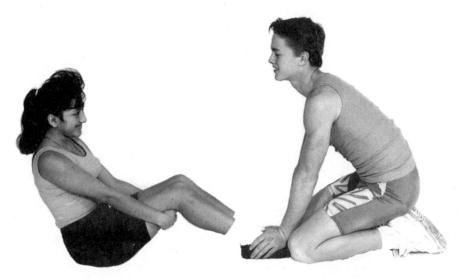

weight up, because the jerk will increase the potential for injury. The weight of your head will be supported by your hands. Don't yank up on the neck muscles. Avoid straining your neck by keeping your eyes focused on the ceiling.

How to do it

1. Lie on your back and clasp your hands behind your neck. Keep your knees bent. Hook your feet under an immovable

object or ask a training partner to hold them to the floor.

2. Slowly sit up. Don't pull on the neck with your clasped hands. Momentarily pause after reaching the sitting position.

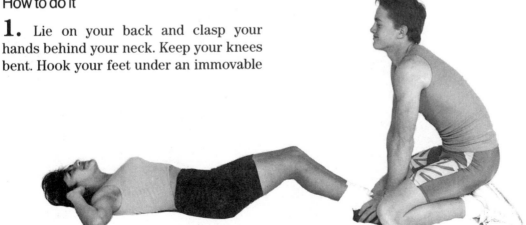

3. Slowly return to the starting position, keeping your knees bent to remove pressure from the back. That's a rep.

Variation

Slant Board Sit-Ups: Sit-ups on a slant board increase the effort required of the abdominal muscles. Form is similar to the regular sit-up.

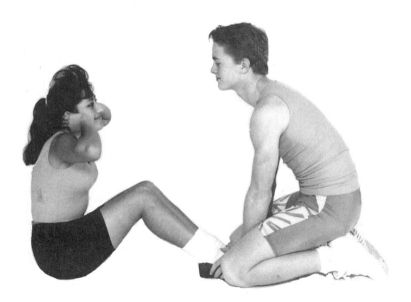

Advanced variation

If you have been practicing sit-ups for quite some time, and are ready to increase the workout, try clasping a light dumbbell behind your head as you perform the basic sit-up.

Chris's Corner

I train my abdominals the same as any other muscles—2 sets of 10 reps. Your stomach muscles might burn after a few sit-ups. That's normal. But if your back muscles start hurting, hold off. Whenever there's pain, stop before it gets worse. And if your back is already hurting from the previous exercises, don't even try these yet.

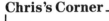

CHEST EXERCISES

Bench Press

Exercise emphasis
- chest
- front of shoulder
- triceps (back of arm)

Equipment needed
- weight bench
- barbell

How to do it

1. Lie on your back with your feet firmly planted on the floor. Space your hands shoulders-width apart. Support the bar at arm's length.

2. Lower the bar toward the chest, keeping the bar under control at all times. Keep your elbows pointed to the sides throughout the movement.

3. Gently touch the bar to the chest approximately an inch above your nipples.

4. Press the bar up until it is again at arm's length. That completes one rep.

Chris's Corner

The bench press is a favorite exercise of mine because it's exciting and very challenging. It builds muscles and strength in my chest, which helps me in track and field when I throw the shot and discus.

Beginners: If you have trouble using a barbell, start with push-ups. Push-ups and bench presses exercise the same muscles. Move from push-ups to the chest bench press as soon as you can do 15 push-ups. At that point you need to advance to the bench press exercise because you no longer have enough body weight for resistance. If you continued increasing the number of push-ups, you would be working for muscular endurance, but by moving to the chest bench press, you will also gain strength.

Regular Push-Up

How to do it

1. Extend your arms below your shoulders. Hold your body rigidly straight.

2. Lower your body until your chest gently touches the floor. Keep your torso and legs in a straight line throughout the movement.

3. Press upward to the starting position keeping your body straight.

Chris's Corner

Don't stick your buttocks up in the air when doing push-ups. Your back should be flat in line with your hips.

Bent-Knee Push-Up

Everything is the same as regular push-ups except that you use the knees as support. Bent-knee push-ups, regular push-ups, and bench presses all work the same muscles.

Chest Fly

Exercise emphasis
- chest
- front of shoulder

Equipment needed
- weight bench
- two dumbbells

Beginners: The chest fly is an awkward movement that requires a spotter for beginners. The spotter should grip the lifter's wrists throughout the entire movement, guiding the path of the arc.

How to do it

1. Lie on your back with your feet firmly planted on the floor and your eyes directed at the ceiling. Hold a dumbbell in each hand, fully extended above your head. Palms should face each other. Hold dumbbells 1 foot apart.

2. Lower the dumbbells through an arc, stopping when the weights fall below shoulder level. Be careful to keep the weight under control throughout the movement.

3. After reaching the lowest point of the arc, slowly move the weight upward through the arc to the starting position. Be sure not to bang the dumbbells together at the top. A finger can find its ways into the middle—ouch! That's a rep.

Chris's Corner _____

This movement doesn't feel natural at the beginning, because it's hard to control. The first time I did the chest fly, I banged my fingers, because it takes a while to learn how to control the dumbbells. Be careful.

Do not bang dumbbells together.

WRONG WAY ☞

SHOULDER EXERCISES

Upright Row

Exercise emphasis

- shoulders
- biceps
- forearms
- neck

Equipment needed

- two dumbbells

Caution: Don't swing or jerk the dumbbells. It accelerates the weight, which interferes with the stress you want your muscles to feel over the full range of the exercise. You can't focus on the muscle groups you're exercising when trying to control a swinging or jerking weight.

How to do it

1. Stand with your feet approximately shoulders-width apart. Hold dumbbells by your thighs.

Don't swing or jerk the dumbbells.

WRONG ☞ WAY

2. Pull your right hand toward your shoulder, keeping the elbow higher than your hand throughout the movement.

3. Lower the dumbbell to the starting position.

Chris's Corner

You'll feel this one! I can sense it in my arms and the front of my shoulders. I do upright rows with 30-pound dumbbells.

Standing Lateral Raise

Exercise emphasis
- shoulders

Equipment needed
- two dumbbells
- weight bench (optional)

How to do it

1. Stand with your feet shoulders-width apart and your knees slightly bent for balance. As an option, you can also perform

4. Perform an identical movement with the left hand, pulling your left hand toward the shoulder. Keep your elbow above your hand throughout the movement.

5. Return your left hand to the starting position. Count 1 rep after you have performed the complete movement with each hand. Alternate right-handed and left-handed movements until you have completed 10 reps. Ten reps is one set.

the exercise lying down. Hold the dumb-bells at arm's length, with your elbows bent about 10 degrees. Palms should face the sides of your thighs.

2. Raise the dumbbells through an arc to the side, retaining the 10-degree bend in the elbows throughout the motion. Keep your palms facing the floor during the arc. End the arc at shoulder height.

3. Lower the weights to the sides of your thighs, following the path of the arc. That's 1 rep.

Chris's Corner

I like this exercise. Try to control the dumbbells both on the way up and the way down. Be careful! Don't bang the weights on your legs.

Chapter 11

Supplementary Exercises

Some people can't get enough of a good thing. Weight trainers fitting that description might want to add one or several supplementary exercises to their workout. The following exercises should not replace any of the basic exercises, described in chapter 10, which were selected to provide a balanced and complete workout for the whole body. If you have the time and energy, however, and want either to accentuate a particular body part or to create a longer overall workout, adding the supplementary exercises can be very beneficial.

Beginners should not add supplementary exercises until they become proficient with the free weights workout. That allows time for the body to acclimate itself to the stresses and nuances of weight training. Jumping into weight training too deeply and too quickly can overwhelm your muscles at the expense of safety; the more prudent approach is to build a strong foundation by learning the basics first.

A word of caution: Don't create an imbalanced body by accentuating one muscle group at the expense of overall development. In other words, don't get so obsessed with developing big biceps that you neglect an equal development of your triceps. You need to work the opposing muscle groups in order to avoid losing joint flexibility. Likewise, don't add a lot of upper body exercises to your training program without adding additional exercises for your legs. You'll look top-heavy.

One goal of a well-designed weight training program is to build a symmetrical, balanced physique that is strong from head to toe. That goal is best met by exercising all parts of the body, being sure to exercise opposing muscle groups at each stop along the way.

With that said, here they are—the supplementary exercises organized according to the muscle group most affected by the exercise.

Chris's Corner

> *If you're like me, once you mastered the basic routine, you were ready for more. Best of all, you can add the exercises that will work the areas you want to improve.*

LEGS

Leg Curl

Exercise emphasis
- back of thigh

Equipment needed
- weight bench

How to do it

1. Lie on a bench or on the floor, face down. Have your training partner grip your ankles.

2. Curl the legs in an arc until your calves touch the backs of your legs. Your training partner supplies the resistance during the movement.

3. Resist as your partner presses your legs to the starting position. That's a rep.

How to do it

1. Position a 2-by-4 or other block on the floor. Hold a dumbbell in your left hand. Stand with your left foot on top of the block. Lean forward, using your right hand for balance. Wrap your right foot around your left ankle.

Standing Toe Raise

Exercise emphasis
- calves

Equipment needed
- a short length of 2-by-4 lumber
- 1 dumbbell

3. Lower through the starting position, stretching your left heel as far toward the floor as possible. That's a rep. Do 9 more with the left leg. Repeat the exercise with the right leg to complete the set.

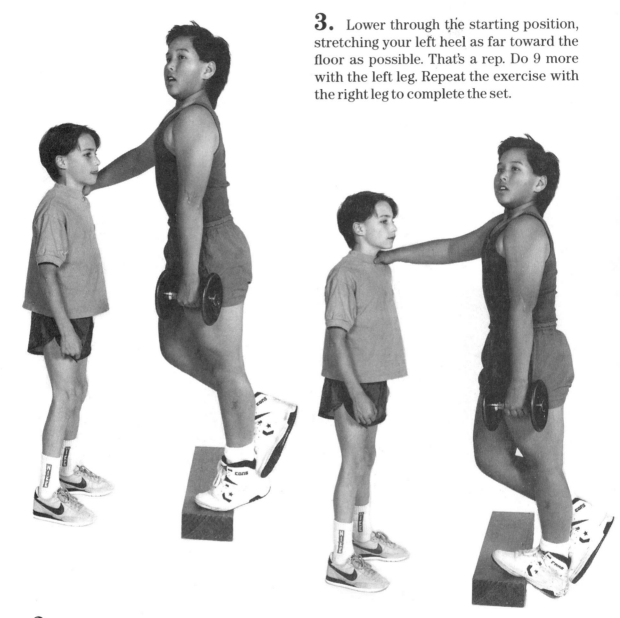

2. Keeping your back straight and your left knee locked, rise up on your left toes as high as you can. Momentarily pause at the top.

CHEST

Dumbbell Press

Equipment needed
- weight bench
- 2 dumbbells

How to do it

1. Lie with your back on a bench, and your feet firmly planted on the floor. With palms facing each other, hold dumbbells at arm's length above your chest. Keep the dumbbells about 6 inches apart.

2. In a controlled movement, lower the dumbbells in straight lines to the sides of the chest; the palms should remain facing each other.

3. Press the dumbbells to the starting position, maintaining the palms-facing position. That's a rep.

Caution: An experienced spotter should hold a beginner's wrists during the movement, to provide balance and stability.

Straight-Armed Dumbbell Pullover

Equipment needed
- weight bench
- 1 dumbbell

How to do it

1. Lie on a bench, your head at the end. Plant feet firmly on the floor. Hold one dumbbell at arm's length above your chest by grasping the bar with both hands; the bar should remain perpendicular to the floor.

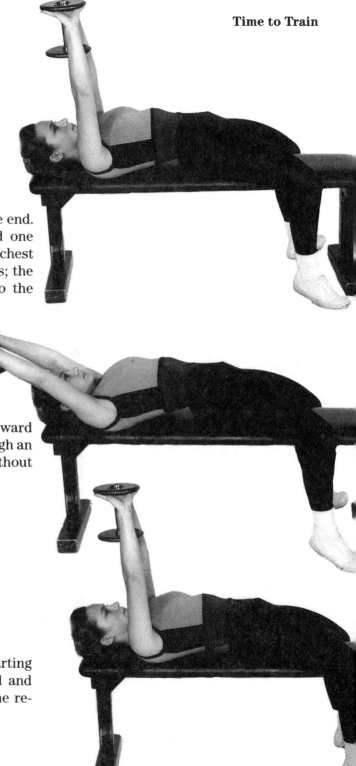

2. Keeping your elbows pointed toward the ceiling, lower the dumbbell through an arc. Reach as far back as possible without pain.

3. Return the dumbbell to the starting position, keeping the elbows locked and pointed toward the ceiling during the return to the top. That's a rep.

SHOULDERS

One-Arm Dumbbell Press

Equipment needed
● 1 dumbbell

Caution: You're lifting a weight overhead. Take care; start light!

How to do it

1. Lift a dumbbell to your right shoulder. With the left hand, grip an immobile object for support and balance. Position feet approximately shoulders-width apart.

Keep the hips, lower back, and legs locked in place.

2. Press the dumbbell to arm's length directly above your shoulder. Pause momentarily at the top.

3. Using control at all times, return the dumbbell to the starting position. That's a rep. Do 9 more with the right arm. Repeat the exercise with your left arm.

Chris's Corner

I had a little trouble balancing the dumbbells when I first tried this exercise. But after a few workouts with a spotter guiding my wrists, I could do them by myself.

Seated Lateral Raise

Equipment needed
- weight bench
- 2 dumbbells

How to do it

1. Sit on the end of a bench, your feet firmly planted on the floor. With palms facing in toward the thighs, hold dumbbells down at your sides.

2. Raise the dumbbells through a lateral arc, keeping your arms straight throughout the movement. Stop when the dumbbells reach shoulder height. The backs of your hands should face the ceiling. Pause momentarily.

3. Lower the dumbbells by returning through the same lateral arc to the starting position. That's a rep.

ARMS

Alternated Dumbbell Curl

Equipment needed
- 2 dumbbells

How to do it

1. Stand with your back straight, legs locked, and feet spaced apart for balance.

Dumbbells should hang at your sides, with your palms facing the thighs.

2. Curl the right hand toward the right shoulder, keeping your elbow close to your side throughout the movement. Allow your wrist to rotate naturally throughout the curl. The palm of the hand will face the shoulder at the top of the movement.

3. Controlling the movement, return the dumbbell to the starting position. That's a rep.

4. After one rep with the right arm, repeat the movement with the left arm, and alternate with each rep. Ten reps with each arm is 1 set.

Variations of the dumbbell curl: seated, alternated seated, and standing positions

Triceps Curl

Equipment needed
- weight bench
- barbell

How to do it

1. Lie on your back, either on a bench or the floor. Grip a barbell with your palms up and your hands spaced about 6 inches apart. Hold the barbell at arm's length above the shoulders.

2. Using control, lower the bar through an arc until the backs of your hands gently touch your forehead. Keep your elbows pointed toward the ceiling throughout the movement.

3. Return through the arc to the starting position, keeping the elbows pointed toward the ceiling. That's a rep.

*Variations of the triceps
curl: standing position*

Hyperextension

Equipment needed
● high, stable bench

How to do it

1. Lie face down, extending your upper body over the end of the bench. Tuck your feet under a support or ask a training partner to hold them. Clasp your hands behind your head.

2. Controlling the movement, bend at the waist, allowing your head to reach as close to the floor as is comfortably possible.

3. Return to the starting position. Hold the starting position for 2 seconds. That's a rep.

Note: This exercise is the only one that is solely for the lower back that the authors recommend. Hyperextensions offer a safe means of strengthening the lower back. Explosive force is not inherent in the movement, and there is no lack of stability if performed on an adequate bench. Most other lower-back exercises fail to address one or both of the foregoing concerns.

NECK

Freehand Neck Resistance

Equipment needed
● none

How to do it

1. While seated, with your eyes focused forward, place your hands on your forehead.

2. Slowly move your head forward while you moderately resist the movement with your hands.

3. Reposition your hands behind your head. Slowly move your head to the rear against the applied resistance of your hands.

4. Place the left hand on the left side of the head. Slowly move your head to the left against the applied resistance of your left hand.

WRONG WAY ☞

5. Repeat the exercise with the right hand by applying pressure to the right side of your head.

Caution: DON'T ASK A TRAINING PARTNER TO APPLY THE RESISTANCE. A neck is an easy thing to injure if too much pressure is applied. You're the best judge of the right amount of pressure to apply without straining your neck.

That's a wrap on supplementary exercises. There are many others, but these exercises were chosen because they are appropriate for kids. In short, they're safe and effective.

Chapter 12

Before Age Eight: Safe Resistance Training for the Very Young

Kids are kids—and they like to play. But remember that although weight training can be fun, it's not a game. Children can do free-play on a jungle gym, but they must conform to the environment of a weight room.

A lot to ask? Yes. But weight training is safe only when safely performed. While there's no magical transformation at eight years old, most kids younger than that don't show the carefulness necessary to participate in a weight training program without endangering themselves.

Developing physical coordination is also a limiting factor for many younger children. Awkwardness keeps some children from correctly performing an exercise, and proper form is essential both for safety and to achieve strength.

Calisthenics, sports, games, and activities such as running, bicycling, and swimming are all vehicles that offer both play and fitness. Resistance training, too, can be done safely—if it is done without weights. The following resistance weight training program is designed to be fun, quick, and safe for the very young boy or girl. With a little assistance from you, they will quickly learn the workout—and be on their way to a lifetime of fitness.

Chris's Corner

You might find out that once you start weight training, your family and friends will want to start too. If they're eight or younger, this is a great program for them.

The five exercises in this resistance training program use the child's body weight as the resistance. No barbells or machines must be mastered. Reliance on balance and coordination is minimized. Yet the exercises build strength, muscular endurance, and flexibility.

Be sure to read chapter 2 (How Weight Training Affects the Prepubescent Body) before helping a child to begin this exercise program. Although that chapter focuses on free weights, the effects of training are comparable when using the body as the resistance.

The following general guidelines for a free-weight training program are equally applicable for the resistance trainer who is eight years old or younger.

Warm up

Emphasize correct form

8 to 10 reps per set

2 sets per exercise

Increase the resistance when you perform more than 10 reps per set.

Push-Up

Exercise emphasis

- chest
- shoulders
- back of arms

(Push-ups work the same muscle groups as free-weight bench presses.)

How to do it

1. Keep your arms straight, and your hands positioned shoulders-width apart with fingers pointing forward.

2. Keeping the body rigidly straight, lower yourself until your chest touches the floor. Don't relax your body at the bottom.

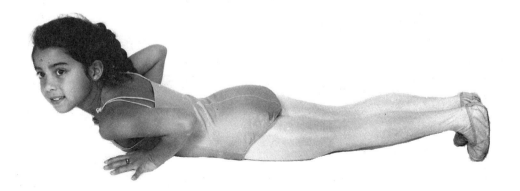

3. Immediately after touching the chest to the floor, push the body back up to the starting position. Down and up is 1 rep.

Variation

Bent-Knee Push-Ups: Bent-knee push-ups supply a smaller resistance to the same movement. Kids who are not yet strong enough for regular push-ups receive the same exercise benefit.

Sit-Up

Exercise emphasis

- abdominals

How to do it

1. Lie on your back with your hands clasped behind your head. Hook your feet

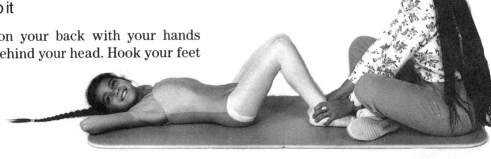

under an immovable object, or have your training partner hold them to the floor.

2. Sit up, trying to touch your head to your knees.

3. Controlling the movement at every stage, lower yourself to the floor and go back to the starting position.

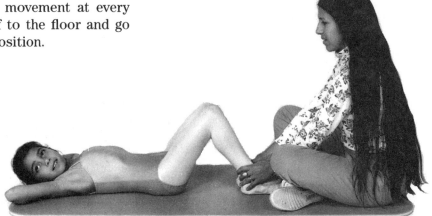

Variation

Easier Sit-Ups: If placing the hands behind your head is too difficult, you can lessen the resistance by placing your hands on your stomach or under your thighs.

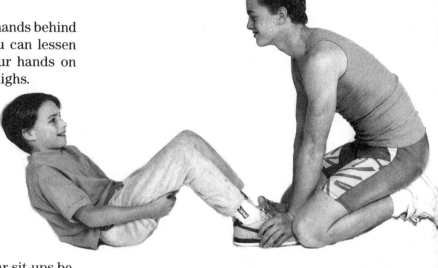

Variation

Inclined Sit-Ups: When regular sit-ups become too easy, do inclined sit-ups. Like the older athlete, you can add resistance by using an incline board.

☞ WRONG WAY

Caution: *Do not pull the neck and head forward with the clasped hands while doing the sit-up. Control the movement with your stomach muscles; don't thrust with your hands and head. You're likely to wake up with a stiff neck the next morning if you do.*

Frog Hop

Exercise emphasis
- upper leg
- lower leg
- hips
- lower back

How to do it

1. Assume a half-squat position, thighs parallel with the floor. The arms should hang at your sides for balance.

2. In one explosive burst, straighten your legs and body and swing your arms up, pushing your body into the air as high as possible. Keep your torso perpendicular to the floor.

3. Continuing the motion, land and drop into the half-squat position.

4. Repeat the movement without pause between reps.

If balance is a problem, a helping hand or bar are okay solutions.

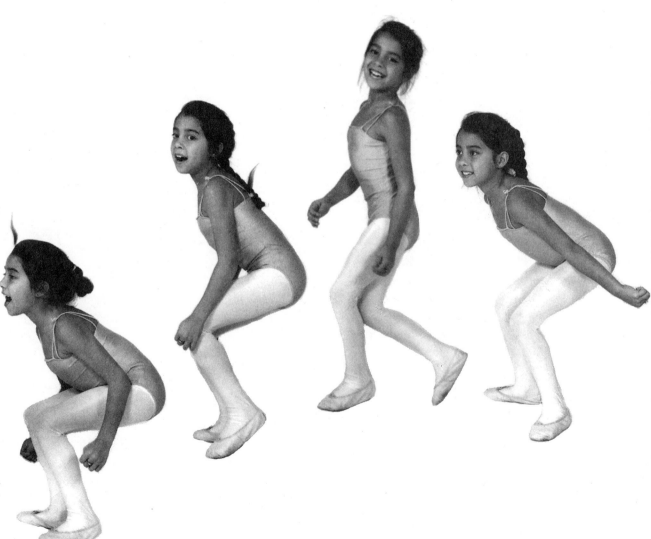

Assisted Pull-Up

Most people, kids or adults, can't do a set of regular pull-ups. The average person has too little pulling strength to complete the exercise without help. We recommend assisted pull-ups, since both versions of pull-ups exercise the same muscle groups.

Exercise emphasis

- upper back
- chest
- shoulders
- biceps
- forearm

How to do it

1. With your hands in an overhand position and spaced shoulders-width apart, hang from the bar. Keep your knees bent and place your feet into the cupped hands of your training partner.

2. Pull yourself up until your chin is level with the bar. While pulling up with your arms, push against your training partner's hands with your feet when you

need to. Don't use the push of your feet more than is absolutely necessary to complete the exercise movement.

3. With control, lower your body to the starting position.

4. Again, don't use the push of your feet any more than you have to.

If you're heavy, pull-ups are more difficult to do.

Leg Raise

Exercise emphasis

- abdominals
- thigh
- hip

How to do it

1. Lie on your back with your hands positioned under your hips, palms down. Bend one knee, with your foot flat on the floor, and extend the other leg.

2. Slowly raise the extended leg to the height of your bent knee.

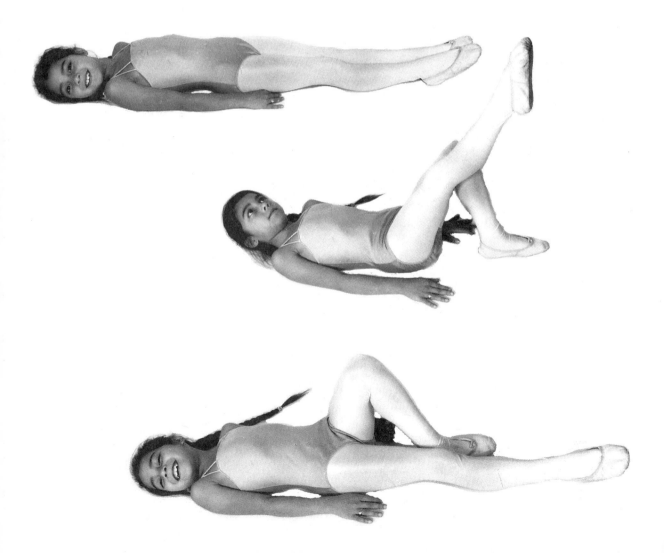

3. Pause momentarily at the top.

4. Slowly lower your leg to the floor, keeping the leg straight throughout the movement.

5. Repeat the movement 10 times with each leg.

Variation

Double-Leg Raise: After you've mastered leg raises with a single leg, you can try a double leg raise.

The above workout should take no more than 30 minutes, but it's a half-hour that can build a safe foundation for future weight training.

Have fun! Before you know it, you'll be pumping iron.

Record-Keeping Charts and Dietary Information

The following charts and tables will help you plan and execute your training program. The reasons for maintaining charts and records can be found in chapter 6 under the heading "Why and how should we keep workout records?"

Diet and exercise progress go hand in hand. The importance of good food and nutrition, as charted in the tables found in this appendix is discussed in chapter 7.

Workout Log

DATE	lunge	step ups	pull ups	dumb-bell rows	sit ups	bench press	chest fly	upright rows	standing lateral raise

Monthly Progress Report

MONTH	lunge	step ups	pull ups	dumb-bell rows	sit ups	bench press	chest fly	upright rows	standing lateral raise

Monthly Measurements

MONTH	BODY WEIGHT	BODY HEIGHT	chest	waist	biceps	thigh	hips	shoulders

Food group	Amount suggested and food included	Nutrients provided
1. Milk or milk products	Children: 3 or more glasses; smaller glasses for children under nine Teenagers: 4 or more glasses (low-fat) Adults: 2 or more glasses (low-fat) 1 cup milk = 1 cup yogurt = 1⅓ oz processed cheddar cheese = 1½ cups cottage cheese = 2 cups ice cream	Protein, fat, carbohydrate Minerals: calcium, phosphorus, magnesium Vitamins: riboflavin, pyridoxine, D and A (if fortified)
2. Meat	2 or more servings (1 serving = 2 to 3 oz cooked lean meat) Meat, poultry, fish, legumes	Protein, fat Minerals: iron, magnesium, phosphorus, zinc Vitamins: B vitamins (cobalamin, folic acid, niacin, pyriodoxine, thiamin)
3. Fruits and vegetables	4 or more servings (1 serving = ½ cup raw or cooked) All fruits and vegetables (include one citrus fruit for vitamin C and one dark green or yellow vegetable for carotene)	Carbohydrate Minerals: calcium and iron (some greens) Vitamins: A (as carotene), B vitamins (folic acid, thiamin), C, E, K
4. Breads and cereals*	4 or more servings (1 serving = 1 slice fortified or whole-grain bread = 1 oz fortified or whole-grain dry cereal = 1 corn tortilla = ½–¾ cup cooked fortified or whole-grain cereal, rice, grits, macaroni, etc.)	Carbohydrate, protein Minerals: iron, magnesium, phosphorus, zinc Vitamins: B vitamins (niacin, pyridoxine, thiamin), E

*Bran, whole-grain breads and cereals, and, to lesser degree, raw and dried fruits and raw vegetables will increase the amount of unabsorbable fiber in the diet.

Source: Diet Manual, University of California at San Francisco Hospitals.

Recommended Dietary Allowances [a]

| | | Weight[b] | | Height[b] | | Protein | Fat-Soluble Vitamins | | | |
| | | | | | | | Vitamin A | Vitamin D | Vitamin E | Vitamin K |
Category	Age (years) or Condition	(kg)	(lb)	(cm)	(in)	(g)	(μ RE)[c]	(μg)[d]	(mgα-TE)[e]	(μ g)
Children	1–3	13	29	90	35	16	400	10	6	15
	4–6	20	44	112	44	24	500	10	7	20
	7–10	28	62	132	52	28	700	10	7	30
Males	11–14	45	99	157	62	45	1,000	10	10	45
	15–18	66	145	176	69	59	1,000	10	10	65
Females	11–14	46	101	157	62	46	800	10	8	45
	15–18	55	120	163	64	44	800	10	8	55

[a] The allowances, expressed as average daily intakes over time, are intended to provide for individual variations among most normal persons as they live in the United States under usual environmental stresses. Diets should be based on a variety of common foods in order to provide other nutrients for which human requirements have been less well defined. See report for detailed discussion of allowances and of nutrients not tabulated.

[b] Weights and heights of reference adults are actual medians for the U.S. population of the designated age, as reported by NHANES II. The median weights and heights of those under 19 years of age were taken from Hamlil et al. (1979). The use of these figures does not imply that the height-to-weight ratios are ideal.

[c] Retinol equivalents. 1 retinol equivalent = 1 μg retinol or 6 μg β-carotene. See report for calculation of vitamin A activity of diets as retinol equivalents. μg = microgram, or one millionth of a gram.

[d] As cholecalciferol. 10 μg cholecalciferol = 400 IU of vitamin D.

[e] α-Tocopherol equivalents. 1 mg d-α tocopherol = 1 α-TE. See report for variation in allowances and calculation of vitamin E activity of the diet as α-tocopherol equivalents.

SOURCE: Food and Nutrition Board, National Academy of Sciences—National Research Council, Washington, D.C.

Recommended Dietary Allowances cont'd

		Water-Soluble Vitamins						
Category	Age (years) or Condition	Vita- min C (mg)	Thia- min (mg)	Ribo- flavin (mg)	Niacin (mg NE)[1]	Vita- min B_6 (mg)	Fo- late (μg)	Vitamin B_{12} (μg)
Children	1–3	40	0.7	0.8	9	1.0	50	0.7
	4–6	45	0.9	1.1	12	1.1	75	1.0
	7–10	45	1.0	1.2	13	1.4	100	1.4
Males	11–14	50	1.3	1.5	17	1.7	150	2.0
	15–18	60	1.5	1.8	20	2.0	200	2.0
Females	11–14	50	1.1	1.3	15	1.4	150	2.0
	15–18	60	1.1	1.3	15	1.5	180	2.0

		Minerals						
Category	Age (years) or Condition	Cal- cium (mg)	Phos- phorus (mg)	Mag- nesium (mg)	Iron (mg)	Zinc (mg)	Iodine (μg)	Sele- nium (μg)
Children	1–3	800	800	80	10	10	70	20
	4–6	800	800	120	10	10	90	20
	7–10	800	800	170	10	10	120	30
Males	11–14	1,200	1,200	270	12	15	150	40
	15–18	1,200	1,200	400	12	15	150	50
Females	11–14	1,200	1,200	280	15	12	150	45
	15–18	1,200	1,200	300	15	12	150	50

1 NE (niacin equivalent) is equal to 1 mg of niacin.

Notes

For more complete publication information, see Bibliography. Numbers in bold face refer to page numbers.

CHAPTER 1: THE BIGGEST QUESTIONS

4. "recent studies show that" Gabe Mirken, *Starting Line*, 10.

4. A series of studies conducted W. Gruchow and P. Pelleiter *American Journal of Sports Medicine*, 234–238.

5. "participation in weight training can result" Jean Barrett Holloway and Thomas R. Baechle, *Sports Medicine*, 216–227.

5. "adversely affect growth, development" Clark Rians et al., *The American Journal of Sports Medicine*, 483–489.

6. "no damage to bone, ephipyses" B. Jacobson and F. Kulling, *The Journal of Orthopaedic and Sports Physical Therapy*, 96–99.

7. weight training is the best exercise B. E. Nilsson and N. E. Westlin, *Clinical Orthopedics and Related Research*, 179–182.

7. boys between the ages of eight and fifteen N. Maffulli, *Sports Medicine*, 229–243.

7. even if a fracture does occur A. M. Pappas, *Physician and Sports Medicine*, 140–146.

10. "Recent studies show that a properly" Gabe Mirken, *Starting Line*, 10.

10. the increased strength acquired L. J. Micheli, *Physician and Sports Medicine*, 25.

11. weight training has no adverse effect Clark Rians, *The American Journal of Sports Medicine*, 483–489.

11. Olympic weight lifters were second only C. Jensen and G. Fisher, *Scientific Basis of Athletic Conditioning*, 208.

11. The range of motion of a joint B. H. Massey and N. L. Chaudet, *Research Quarterly*, 41–51.

CHAPTER 2: HOW WEIGHT TRAINING AFFECTS THE PREPUBESCENT BODY

17. a 42-percent strength increase L. J. Micheli, *Physician and Sports Medicine*, 25.

17. ten-percent initial increases in strength K. Hakkinen, *National Strength and Conditioning Association Journal*, 32–37.

17. gains in strength are reportedly the same J. A. Siegal, D. N. Camaione, and T. Manfredi, *Pediatric Exercise Science*, 145–154.

17. a 48-percent gain in strength Alfred Roncarati, *Track and Field Quarterly Review*, 40–42.

17. "recent investigations overwhelmingly support" B. Jacobson and F. Kulling, *The Journal of Orthopedic and Sports Physical Therapy*, 96–99.

17. the primary underlying mechanism D. G. Sale, *Perspectives in Exercise Science and Sports Medicine*, 165–216.

19. blood level of GH rises as much as 260 percent W. P. Vanhelder, M. W. Radomski, and R. C. Goode, *European Journal of Applied Physiology and Occupational Physiology*, 31–34.

19. supervised weight training is safe for children American Academy of Pediatrics policy statement and National Strength and Conditioning Association position paper, 27–31.

CHAPTER 3: WEIGHT TRAINING AND THE JOURNEY THROUGH PUBERTY

21. concludes puberty with 13-percent body fat C. L. Wells and S. A. Plowman, *Physician and Sports Medicine*, 53–63.

23. "unit for unit, female muscle tissue" Jean Barrett Holloway and Thomas R. Baechle, *Sports Medicine*, 216–227.

24. 262,000 students . . . have used steroids Marlene Cimons, *Los Angeles Times*.

26. average male is 10-percent taller C. L. Wells and S. A. Plowman, *Physician and Sports Medicine*, 53–63.

27. intense training elevates the blood testosterone National Strength and Conditioning Association Women's Position Paper Committee, *NSCA Journal*, 43–56.

27. "Coaches don't really know" Lawrie Woodman, *Sports Coach*, 18–21.

CHAPTER 4: GUIDANCE AND CAMARADERIE: ESTABLISHING RAPPORT BETWEEN ADULTS AND KIDS

31. "children are encultured to view" Jean Barrett Holloway and Thomas R. Baechle, *Sports Medicine*, 216–227.

34. nearly half of all boys Scott Roberts, *American Fitness Quarterly*, 18–20.

CHAPTER 8: WEIGHT TRAINING AND NUTRITION

63. most often the result of lifting J. R. Ryan and G. G. Salciccioli, *The American Journal of Sports Medicine*, 26–27.

64. "The load utilized in performing resistance" William J. Kraemer, A. C. Fry, P. N. Frykman, B. Conroy, and J. Hoffman, *Pediatric Exercise Science*, 336–351.

64. vast majority of exercise injuries F. L. Allman, *Athletic Journal*, 74.

65. quick lifts are the most conducive M. J. L. Alexander, *Canadian Journal of Applied Sports Sciences*, 1–20.

Bibliography

Alexander, M.J.L. "Biomechanical Aspects of Lumbar Spine Injuries in Athletes: A Review." *Canadian Journal of Applied Sports Sciences* 10.1 (1985): 1–20.

Allman, F. L. "Prevention of Sports Injuries." *Athletic Journal* 56.7 (1976): 74.

American Academy of Pediatrics' Committee on Sports Medicine Policy Statment: "Strength Training, Weight and Power Lifting, and Body Building by Children and Adolescents." (1989): unpublished.

Gruchow, W., and Pelleiter, P. "An Epidemiologic Study of Tennis Elbow." *American Journal of Sports Medicine* 7 (1979): 234–238.

Hakkinen, K. "Factors Influencing Trainability of Muscular Strength During Short-Term and Prolonged Training." *National Strength and Conditioning Association Journal* 2 (1985): 32–37.

Holloway, J.B., and Baechle, T. R. "Strength Training for Female Athletes: A Review of Selected Aspects." *Sports Medicine* 9.4 (1990): 216–227.

Jacobson, B., and Kulling, F. "Effect of Resistive Weight Training in Prepubescents." *The Journal of Orthopaedic and Sports Physical Therapy* 11.3 (1989): 96–99.

Jensen, C., and Fisher, G. *Scientific Basis of Athletic Conditioning.* Philadelphia: Lea and Febiger, 1979.

Kraemer, W. J.; Fry, A. C.; Frykman, P. N.; Conroy, B.; and Hoffman, J. "Resistance Training and Youth." *Pediatric Exercise Science* 1.4 (1989): 336–351.

Maffulli, N. "Intensive Training in Young Athletes: The Orthopaedic Surgeon's Viewpoint." *Sports Medicine* 9.4 (1990): 229–243.

Massey, B. H., and Chaudet, N. L. "Effects of Heavy Resistance Exercise on Range of Joint Movement in Young Male Adults." *Re-*

search Quarterly 27 (1956): 41–51.

Micheli, L. J. "Strength Gains in Preadolescents." *Physician and Sports Medicine* 11 (1983): 25.

Mirken, G. "Strength Training Before Puberty." *Starting Line* 18.1 (Summer 1990): 10.

National Strength and Conditioning Association. "Position Paper on Prepubescent Strength Training." *National Strength and Conditioning Association Journal* 7.4 (1986): 27–31.

National Strength and Conditioning Association Women's Position Paper Committee. "Official Document: Strength Training for Female Athletes: A Position Paper: Part I." *National Strength and Conditioning Association Journal* 11.4 (1989): 43–56.

Nilsson, B. E., and Westlin, N. E. "Bone Density in Athletes." *Clinical Orthopedics and Related Reserach* 7 (1971): 179–182.

Pappas, A. M. "Epiphyseal Injuries in Sports." *Physician and Sports Medicine* 11.6 (1983): 140–146.

Rians, C. et al. "Strength Training for Prepubescent Males: Is It Safe?" *The American Journal of Sports Medicine* 15.5 (1987): 483–489.

Roberts, S. "Assessing the Fitness Needs of Youth." *American Fitness Quarterly* (April 1990): 18–20.

Roncarati, A. "Prepubescent Strength Training: Is It Worth the Effort?" *Track and Field Quarterly Review* (Fall 1988): 40–42.

Ryan, J. R., and Salciccioli, G. G. "Fractures of the Distal Radial Epiphysis in Adolescent Weight Lifters." *The American Journal of Sports Medicine* 4 (1976): 26–27.

Sale, D. G. "Strength Training in Children." Report in *Perspectives in Exercise Science and Sports Medicine.* Edited by C. V. Gisolfi and D. R. Lamb, Benchmark Press (1989): 165–216.

Siegal, J. A.; Camaione, D. N.; and Manfredi, T. G. "The Effects of Upper Body Resistance Training on Prepubescent Children." *Pediatric Exercise Science* 1.2 (1989): 145–154.

Vanhelder, W. P.; Radomski, M. W.; and Goode, R. C. "Growth Hormone Responses During Intermittent Weight Lifting Exercise in Men." *European Journal of Applied Physiology and Occupational Physiology* 53 (1984): 31–34.

Wells, C. L., and Plowman, S. A. "Sexual Differences in Athletic Performance." *Physician and Sports Medicine* 11.8 (1983): 53–63.